Hybrid AI Frameworks for Intelligent Video Surveillance Systems

Yahya

Table of Contents

1

INTRODUCTION

University campuses are dynamic environments that demand continuous and intelligent surveillance to ensure safety. Traditional CCTV systems, though widely deployed, are limited by manual monitoring, poor real-time responsiveness, and low accuracy in challenging conditions such as low lighting, crowd occlusion, or unusual movement. This research aims to design an AI-powered, hybrid, real-time surveillance system tailored specifically for university campuses, incorporating person identification and behavior analysis.

1.1 Background of the Study

In recent years, the need for enhanced campus security has grown due to increasing concerns over unauthorized access, behavioral anomalies, and safety violations in educational institutions. Traditional surveillance systems, although widely deployed, rely heavily on human monitoring, which is prone to fatigue, inconsistency, and delayed response.

Advancements in Artificial Intelligence (AI) and Computer Vision (CV) have paved the way for intelligent surveillance systems capable of real-time detection, recognition, and interpretation of human activities. Integrating these technologies into university campus monitoring offers the potential to automate threat detection, streamline identity verification, and recognize behavioral patterns proactively.

Particularly, the synergy of deep learning algorithms like YOLO (Redmon et al. (2016); Daasan & Ishak (2024), CNNs (Goodfellow et al. 2016), LSTM (Hochreiter & Schmidhuber 1997) and super-resolution techniques (like ESRGAN) Wang et al. (2019) enables a more robust analysis even on low-resolution CCTV footage. Further FaceNet (Schroff et al. 2015) embeddings and Deep SVM classifiers (Vapnik 1999) empower accurate person identification. These AI components collectively enhance campus security through real-time analysis, alert generation, and actionable insights, making campuses not only safer but smarter.

1.2 Statement of the Problem

Conventional surveillance systems deployed in most university campuses are:

- Heavily reliant on human observation.
- Limited by low-resolution footage.
- Incapable of real-time identity recognition.
- Lacking behavior analysis features.

Moreover, the sheer volume of video data generated across a campus makes it impractical for manual review and monitoring. The absence of intelligent automation leads to delayed responses, overlooked incidents, and compromised safety. There is a pressing need for a system that:

- Can automatically detect individuals and activities of interest.
- Works reliably with low-quality video inputs.
- Provides real-time, context-aware alerts.
- Adheres to ethical and legal standards in educational contexts.

1.3 Objectives of the Research

- to enhance the low-quality surveillance footage, to improve the visibility of facial and body features in low-resolution or poorly illuminated real time video frames since surveillance cameras often capture noisy or low-resolution footage, especially in the dark.

- to enhance face detection process for robust, accurate, and real-time detection of faces in surveillance videos *even under challenging conditions such as occlusions, motion blur or poor lighting.*
- to enhance temporal and contextual patterns of movement of individuals to detect abnormal or suspicious behavior.
- to enhance *the person* identification process that accurately identifies individuals.
- to *compare the results* achieved through Traditional methods and the innovative Hybrid method.

1.4 Significance of the Study

This research is significant both technically and socially:

- Technological Impact: Demonstrates the integration of multiple AI techniques into a unified, real-time, modular surveillance framework suitable for real-world deployment.
- Security Enhancement: Improves the safety of students, faculty, and staff by automating threat detection and rapid incident response.
- Scalability: Offers a blueprint for deploying AI surveillance in other critical public spaces such as hospitals, libraries, or urban zones.
- Academic Contribution: Provides a reference implementation for future research in intelligent surveillance systems.
- Ethical Considerations: Promotes responsible AI use by incorporating GDPR guidelines and ethical surveillance practices.

1.5 Overview of the Thesis Structure

This thesis is systematically structured into seven chapters to present a comprehensive view of the development, implementation, and evaluation of a hybrid AI-powered surveillance system for university campuses. Each chapter builds upon the previous one, ensuring a logical progression from foundational concepts to technical realization and performance validation.

Chapter1 establishes the background, motivation, problem statement, research objectives, and the significance of deploying intelligent surveillance in educational environments.

Chapter 2 reviews prior work on face and behavior detection, surveillance systems, object recognition algorithms, and hybrid model implementations, identifying key research gaps, introduces core concepts related to artificial intelligence, computer vision, and their role in campus security. It also categorizes the classical and deep learning models relevant to the research, discusses classical methods such as Viola-Jones and HOG+SVM, their mathematical foundations, feature extraction techniques, and inherent limitations in modern surveillance, discusses the detailed state-of-the-art deep learning techniques including CNNs, SSD, and YOLO (versions 5 to 8), elaborating on their internal mechanisms, performance trade-offs, and detection accuracy, explores the ESRGAN model for improving the quality of low-resolution surveillance frames, explaining its architecture, training dynamics, and impact on downstream detection, covers the RAFT model for dense optical flow and LSTM networks for temporal sequence learning to enable motion tracking and behavior classification, focuses on identity recognition through FaceNet embeddings and classification using Deep Support Vector Machines (SVM), including decision boundaries and similarity measures, presents the end-to-end real-time surveillance pipeline from video capture to alert generation, supported by modular Python implementation and deployment guidelines.

Chapter 3 outlines the step-by-step approach followed in model selection, system design, integration of algorithms, dataset preparation, and evaluation strategy, describes the layered architecture of the proposed system, highlighting the data flow, module interaction, and hardware/software components, gives the details of the process of video collection, annotation, preprocessing, augmentation, and structuring for training and evaluating each model layer, introduces the fusion framework integrating multiple models for detection, behavior analysis, and identity recognition. It explains the rationale behind model hybridization, fusion engine design, and mathematical logic for decision-level integration.

Chapter 4 evaluates the system using metrics like precision, recall, F1-score, inference speed (FPS), and latency. It also compares individual models with the hybrid model under various real-world conditions such as occlusion and low light.

Chapter 5 discusses the interpretation of results, compares with existing literature and implies the findings.

Chapter 6 discusses GDPR compliance, data privacy policies, ethical issues in deploying facial recognition in academic settings, and the role of human oversight in automated alert systems.

Chapter 7 summarizes the research findings, discusses the significance of the hybrid surveillance model, and outlines directions for future enhancements including edge computing, multimodal biometrics, and explainable AI.

1.6 Fundamentals Of AI-Based Video Surveillance

Artificial Intelligence (AI) is transforming conventional surveillance systems into intelligent, real-time monitoring platforms that can autonomously detect threats, identify individuals, and analyze behavior (Rashid et al., 2019; Kortli et al., 2020). In campus environments where student and staff safety, asset protection, and incident prevention are paramount AI plays a critical role in ensuring proactive security (Mann & Smith, 2017; Smith & Miller, 2022).

1.6.1 Overview of AI in Campus Surveillance

Modern university campuses are dynamic and spatially dispersed, often making it infeasible for human operators to continuously monitor multiple video feeds. AI enhances surveillance through automation of routine tasks like face detection, person tracking, and anomaly detection. It also reduces dependency on manual oversight and increases responsiveness by generating alerts in real time (Rashid et al., 2019; Kortli et al., 2020).

Key applications of AI in campus surveillance include:

- Intruder detection in restricted areas (Rashid et al., 2019).
- Attendance automation using facial recognition (Sajid et al., 2014; Jadhav et al., 2024).
- Tracking suspicious activities such as loitering or aggressive behavior (Zhou, 2020).
- Missing person detection via face matching across multiple camera feeds (Kortli et al., 2020).

The integration of AI enables campuses to shift from reactive to proactive security paradigms, thus significantly improving institutional safety and decision-making (Rashid et al., 2019; Smith & Miller, 2022).

1.6.2 Basics of Computer Vision and AI in Security

Computer Vision (CV)is a subfield of AI that enables computers to interpret visual data from the real world such as images and videos for understanding, reasoning, and action. In surveillance, CV is used to process and analyze live video streams to identify people, track movement, and detect behavioral patterns.

Key Components of AI-CV Surveillance:

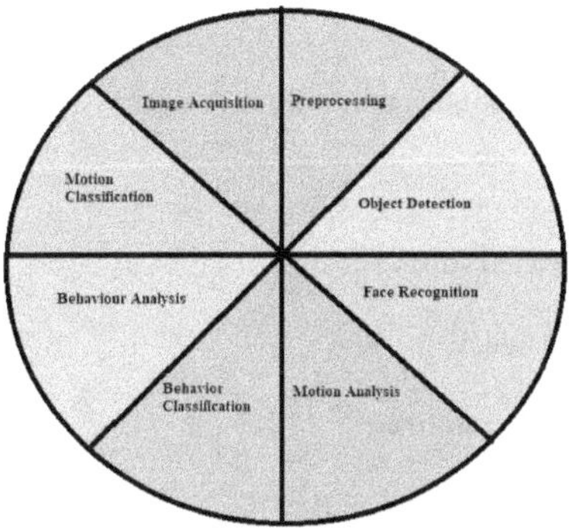

Figure 1.1: Key Components of AI-CV Surveillance

Computer Vision tasks are generally divided into spatial analysis (e.g., detecting where a person is) and temporal analysis (e.g., understanding what they are doing over time).

1.6.3 Overview of Person Detection, Recognition, and Behavior Analysis

AI-based surveillance systems operate through a series of coordinated sub-tasks:

a) Person Detection

This refers to identifying and locating human figures in video frames. It includes:

- Face detection (e.g., Viola-Jones)
- Full-body detection (e.g., HOG + SVM)
- Multi-scale detection using SSD or YOLO

b) Person Recognition

Once a face is detected, it is compared against a stored database to determine identity. Steps include:

- Feature extraction using deep networks like FaceNet
- Embedding generation for faces
- Classification using Deep SVM or cosine similarity

c) Behavior Analysis

This involves analyzing the temporal patterns of movement to detect:

- Suspicious loitering
- Trespassing into restricted zones
- Unusual gait or group behavior

Behavior recognition typically requires:

- Motion features from RAFT (optical flow)
- Temporal modeling using LSTM

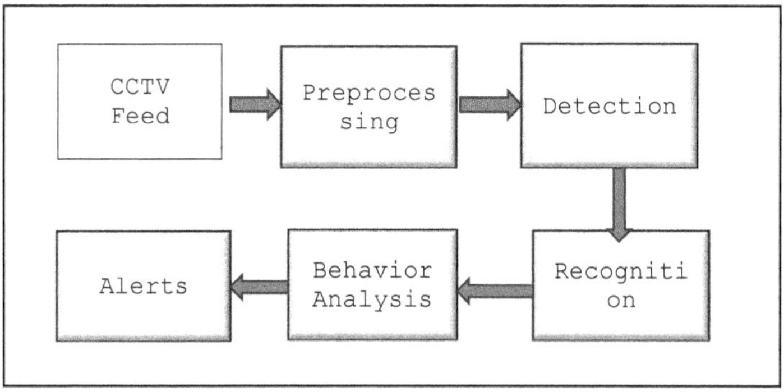

Figure1.2: Modular Pipeline

1.6.4 Taxonomy of Classical and Deep Learning Models

AI models used in surveillance can be categorized into classical machine learning and deep learning models, each having unique strengths and limitations.

A. Classical Models

Model	Description	Applications
Viola - Jones	Haar-like features + cascading classifiers	Fast face detection
HOG + SVM	Gradient-based descriptors + linear classifiers	Pedestrian/human body detection
PCA / LDA	Dimensionality reduction, face matching	Early face recognition techniques

Table 1.1: Classical Models

These models are computationally efficient but struggle under variable lighting, occlusions, or large datasets.

B. Deep Learning Models

Model	Description	Strengths
CNN	Learns spatial hierarchies of features	High accuracy for feature extraction
SSD	Single-pass multi-scale detector	Real-time object/person detection
YOLOv5/YOLOv12	Grid-based detectors with speed-accuracy optimization	Multi-object, high-speed detection
FaceNet	Embedding-based face recognition using triplet loss	Robust against pose and lighting
RAFT	Dense optical flow estimation for motion tracking	Accurate trajectory estimation
LSTM	Recurrent neural network for sequence modeling	Behavior recognition over time
Deep SVM	Non-linear classification of high-dimensional face embeddings	Identity classification

Table1.2: Deep Learning Models

C. Why Hybridization?

No single model (Rashid et al., 2019; Wang & Deng, 2021) performs optimally under all conditions. Hence, hybrid models integrate:

- Traditional methods for speed and fallback
- Deep models for accuracy and adaptability
- Motion models for contextual understanding
- Fusion engines for decision-level optimization

This layered strategy allows AI surveillance systems to handle diverse challenges, such as occlusion, low resolution, varying angles, and unpredictable behavior.

2

LITERATURE SURVEY

2.1 Introduction

This literature review serves as a foundational pillar of any academic research work. It establishes the theoretical and empirical grounding of the study by critically analyzing and synthesizing existing work in the domain. This chapter presents a comprehensive review of scholarly contributions in the fields of artificial intelligence (AI), computer vision, facial recognition, video surveillance, behavior analysis, and deep learning, particularly focusing on their applications in campus security systems.

The overarching objective of this chapter is to examine how existing technologies have evolved to meet the growing demands for intelligent surveillance and person identification. By doing so, it also helps identify key limitations, gaps, and opportunities that shape the direction of the current research. The review draws from a rich array of sources, including peer-reviewed journal articles, conference proceedings, benchmark datasets, and cutting-edge methodologies proposed over the last three decades.

Purpose of the Literature Review

The main purposes of this literature review are:

- **To contextualize the research problem**: By tracing the evolution of facial recognition and surveillance technologies, the chapter provides context for the emergence of AI-powered campus security solutions.

- **To survey and evaluate existing technologies**: This includes traditional methods like HOG + SVM and PCA, as well as advanced deep learning techniques such as CNNs, YOLO models, FaceNet, ESRGAN, and RAFT.
- **To identify research gaps and limitations**: Although extensive work has been conducted on individual components like face recognition and behavior detection, few studies focus on **unified, real-time surveillance pipelines** customized for academic environments.
- **To justify the need for hybrid surveillance systems**: The integration of enhancement (ESRGAN), detection (YOLO), motion tracking (RAFT), temporal modeling (LSTM), and classification (SVM) is necessary for improving surveillance accuracy and responsiveness.

2.2 Traditional Approaches to Face Detection and Recognition Algorithms

Before the rise of deep learning, traditional face detection and recognition techniques formed the backbone of computer vision systems. These methods primarily relied on **hand-crafted features**, **statistical pattern recognition**, and **shallow machine learning algorithms**. Though constrained by variations in lighting, pose, and occlusion (Delac et al., 2005; Kortli et al., 2020), these early models laid essential groundwork for the development of modern facial recognition systems.

This section presents a detailed review of foundational algorithms and techniques used in traditional face detection and recognition, including the Viola-Jones framework, HOG + SVM, and various statistical and appearance-based methods such as PCA, LDA, ICA, LBP, and HMM (Martinez & Kak, 2001; Shan et al., 2009; Nefian & Hayes, 1998).

2.3 Viola-Jones Algorithm (Viola & Jones, 2001)

The **Viola-Jones face detection algorithm** was the first framework to enable **real-time face detection** and remains a milestone in computer vision. Its major components include:

- **Haar-like features**: Simple rectangular features representing intensity differences between regions in an image.
- **Integral image**: A fast computation method allowing rapid summation of pixel values in rectangular regions.
- **AdaBoost classifier**: Used to select a small number of critical features and build a strong classifier from weak learners.
- **Cascade structure**: A multi-stage pipeline that quickly rejects non-face regions and efficiently allocates computation to promising face candidates.

This method is highly efficient and computationally lightweight, making it ideal for embedded systems. However, it performs poorly under significant variations in face orientation, lighting, and occlusion.

The **Viola-Jones** algorithm, introduced in 2001, is one of the earliest and fastest real-time face detection methods. It employs a set of rectangular Haar-like features and a boosted cascade of classifiers. The Viola-Jones algorithm is often seen as the foundation of modern face detection systems. Its biggest breakthrough was its ability to detect faces in real-time, even on limited computing devices, such as early webcams or security cameras.

2.3.1 Haar-like Features, Integral Images, AdaBoost

Haar-like Features:

Imagine placing white and black tiles over an image and checking if there's a difference in brightness. That's the idea behind Haar features. For instance:

- The area between one's eyes is usually darker than one's cheeks.
- The eye region is often darker than the bridge of the nose.

Haar-like features capture these types of visual contrasts.

Integral Image

Normally, checking these brightness differences pixel-by-pixel would take a long time. The integral image is like a shortcut a quick cheat sheet that allows the system to look at any section of the image almost instantly. This innovation made face detection incredibly fast.

Haar features are rectangular features that resemble convolution filters and capture edge, line, and corner structures in grayscale images.

Example:

- Two-rectangle feature: detects vertical edges.
- Three-rectangle feature: detects lines.

AdaBoost:

In the Viola-Jones face detection framework; the algorithm generates an enormous number of Haar-like features from even a small image window. While these features capture important patterns such as the contrast between eye sockets and cheeks not all of them are equally useful. Processing every single one would be computationally expensive and inefficient. This is where AdaBoost, or Adaptive Boosting, plays a crucial role. Acting like a smart and selective coach, AdaBoost scans through the vast pool of features and identifies only those that consistently contribute to successful face detection. By choosing the most effective features, it trims down the system to focus only on what truly matters, making the overall process both faster and more accurate.

Beyond just selecting good features, AdaBoost also can adapt to difficult detection scenarios. During training, if certain faces are frequently misclassified perhaps due to variations in lighting, angle, or partial occlusion, AdaBoost automatically adjusts by assigning these difficult examples greater importance. This means that the algorithm gives extra attention to faces that are hard to detect, thereby learning how to improve its accuracy in handling real-world complexity. In effect, the model becomes more robust over time by focusing its learning efforts on its past mistakes.

Another remarkable feature of AdaBoost is its ability to turn multiple weak classifiers into a single strong decision-making system. A weak classifier, in this context, is a feature that performs only slightly better than random guessing. While individually limited, when several of these weak classifiers are combined each given a weight based on its reliability they create a powerful ensemble. AdaBoost coordinates this combination, assigning higher confidence to more dependable features and letting their collective output determine whether a face is present in each image region. The result is a well-balanced system that performs significantly better than any of the individual classifiers on their own.

Not all Haar features are useful. AdaBoost is like a coach who watches hundreds of face detection attempts and says, "Let's focus only on the features that help most."

2.3.2 Cascaded Classifier Architecture

One of the most innovative aspects of the Viola-Jones face detection algorithm is its use of a cascaded classifier architecture. This structure significantly enhances the efficiency and speed of detection, making it suitable for real-time applications such as digital cameras, CCTV systems, and embedded security devices.

The idea behind a cascade is straightforward but powerful: not all regions in an image are equally likely to contain a face. So instead of analyzing every part of the image with the same intensity, the algorithm processes image regions through a series of increasingly complex checks. The initial stages, or early layers of the cascade, use a small number of simple features to quickly eliminate obvious non-facial areas. These early checks act like rough filters swiftly rejecting regions that don't resemble a face at all, such as blank walls or furniture.

If a region passes this initial screening, it progresses to the next stage of the cascade, where more complex and refined features are applied. These later stages delve deeper, performing a more detailed analysis on only those regions that have a higher chance of containing a face. Each stage is trained to either reject or pass regions based on the confidence that a face might be present. This progressive filtering greatly reduces unnecessary computations because most of the image is ruled out early, and only a few promising regions are evaluated in full detail.

This architectural design results in exceptional processing speed, which is one of the reasons why Viola-Jones gained popularity in the early 2000s. It was one of the first face detection systems fast enough to run on limited hardware, making it ideal for mobile devices, low-resolution surveillance feeds, and embedded systems. Its ability to detect faces at 15-30 frames per second enabled real-time applications that were previously impractical.

However, despite its strengths, the cascaded classifier architecture has certain limitations. Since it was designed with speed as a priority, it assumes that faces are frontal, upright, and well-lit. As a result, the system struggles when faces are partially covered (occluded), rotated, or captured in poor lighting conditions. It also finds it challenging to detect faces at extreme angles or when facial expressions deviate significantly from neutral. These shortcomings become evident in more dynamic or crowded environments such as public spaces or outdoor settings, where faces may not appear in a standardized form.

The cascaded classifier architecture is a clever and efficient way of prioritizing computational resources investing time and effort only where it is likely to yield a successful detection. It remains a valuable technique in situations where speed and simplicity are paramount, though it has largely been surpassed in accuracy by more recent deep learning models that can handle greater visual variation.

The cascade architecture works like a multi-layer security checkpoint:

1. First gate: Quickly eliminates obvious non-face areas.
2. Second gate: Takes a closer look at what's left.
3. Final gates: Perform detailed checks only where necessary.

This layered approach makes it extremely fast and efficient, especially when scanning large video frames or real-time footage.

Example in Campus Surveillance:

In a university CCTV system, Viola-Jones could be used to quickly scan corridors or entrances to detect faces of students entering buildings. Its speed is beneficial when processing many camera feeds at once.

Challenges:

- Missing faces that are tilted, partially hidden, or poorly lit.
- Struggles in low-light or outdoor environments without uniform lighting.

2.4 Histogram of Oriented Gradients (HOG) + SVM

The Histogram of Oriented Gradients (HOG) combined with a Support Vector Machine (SVM) classifier is a well-established method for detecting humans, faces, and other structured objects in images. Introduced by Dalal and Triggs in 2005, this approach became a foundational technique in computer vision, especially for tasks such as pedestrian detection before the rise of deep learning (Dalal & Triggs, 2005; Kortli et al., 2020).

At its core, the HOG technique works by focusing not on the color or brightness of an image, but on the shape and edges, that is, where the image changes most sharply (Dalal & Triggs, 2005). In real-world terms, if you imagine looking at a photograph in black and white, one's eye is naturally drawn to edges, like where a face begins against a background or where shadows define the nose and eyes. HOG tries to capture this type of visual information by breaking an image into small cells and measuring how the edges (or gradients) within each cell are oriented (Dalal & Triggs, 2005).

Instead of trying to understand what an object is pixel by pixel, HOG simplifies the image by creating a histogram (a kind of summary chart) of which directions the edges are pointing in each part of the image. This provides a compact representation of the overall shape and contour of objects, which is especially useful when detecting faces or bodies, as these shapes are generally consistent even when details vary (Shan et al., 2009).

Once these HOG features are extracted from an image, they are passed into a Support Vector Machine (SVM). This is a type of classifier that acts like a boundary-setter: it learns from examples of faces and non-faces and figures out where to draw the line that separates them. The SVM (Weston & Watkins, 1999) uses these examples to recognize new patterns by determining whether a new set of HOG features looks more like a face or not.

This two-step process first extracting structured shape information using HOG, then classifying it with SVM proved highly effective in its time. It offered a balance between speed and accuracy, making it useful for early applications like security monitoring, vehicle-based pedestrian detection, and real-time face tracking in lower-resource systems (Bakshi & Singhal, 2014).

The HOG + SVM approach was particularly celebrated for being interpretable, meaning that developers and researchers could understand how it worked internally unlike today's deep learning models, which often operate as black boxes (Wanyonyi & Celik, 2022). Additionally, it did not require large datasets to train, making it accessible for smaller projects or situations where labeled data was limited (Kortli et al., 2020).

However, like the Viola-Jones method, HOG + SVM has its limitations (Viola & Jones, 2001). It typically struggles with images that involve complex backgrounds, occlusions, low contrast, or where the subject is not clearly defined (Delac et al., 2005). In such cases, more flexible and robust models like convolutional neural networks (CNNs) perform significantly better (Wang & Deng, 2021).

In summary, the HOG + SVM framework is a classic and influential model that laid the groundwork for more modern techniques. It introduced an effective way to represent shapes in images and combined that with a reliable classifier to detect objects. Even though it has been largely replaced by deep learning in recent years, it remains a key milestone in the evolution of computer vision (Wanyonyi & Celik, 2022).

2.4.1 Gradient Computation and Orientation Bins

The first and most important step in the Histogram of Oriented Gradients (HOG) method is understanding how the image changes in intensity across different directions what we call the gradient. A gradient, in simple terms, tells us where and how strongly the image changes. For example, in a photo, the edge of a face or the border between a light area and a shadow is where the most significant changes happen. These changes are what HOG tries to capture.

To detect these changes, the algorithm looks at each pixel in the image and examines how the brightness shifts in the surrounding pixels both horizontally and vertically. It doesn't care about the color or texture itself but rather how quickly and in what direction the image goes from light to dark. This allows the system to find edges and shapes, which are very important for identifying objects like faces or people.

Once the gradients (i.e., the directions and strengths of brightness changes) are computed for every pixel, the image is divided into small rectangular sections called cells typically 8×8 pixels each. Within each of these cells, the algorithm counts how many pixels have gradient directions pointing in specific ranges such as vertical, diagonal, or horizontal. These counts are organized into a kind of bar chart or histogram representing the orientation of edges in that region.

However, to make the system more resilient to changes in lighting or contrast, the algorithm doesn't just look at one cell at a time. It groups a few neighboring cells together into larger regions called blocks usually covering 2×2 cells. These blocks serve as units for normalization, a process that ensures the detected edge patterns are consistent regardless of how bright or dark the image is. For instance, a person walking under a shadow or in sunlight would still have similar edge patterns, and normalization helps the system recognize them equally well.

In essence, this process creates a detailed map of the image's structure highlighting the direction of edges across the image in a way that is independent of lighting conditions. The result is a compact and highly descriptive feature set that captures the shape and geometry of the object being analyzed, which is then passed to a classifier like SVM for final detection.

This clever breakdown of edge directions, combined with lighting normalization, is what made HOG particularly effective for detecting faces, pedestrians, and other structured objects long before deep learning took over.

Gradients:

Gradients are changes in brightness between neighboring pixels. Wherever there's a strong change like along the edge of a face, shoulder, or leg that's a good place to understand the object's shape.

2.4.2 Feature Extraction and Classification with SVM

After computing gradient orientations and organizing them into histograms within each block of the image, the next step in the HOG + SVM pipeline is to convert this information into a usable format for classification. This process is called feature extraction (Dalal & Triggs, 2005).

Think of feature extraction as turning an image into a list of numbers that summarize its visual structure. Each block of the image containing edge directions and magnitudes is represented as a vector (Dalal & Triggs, 2005), like a fingerprint of that part of the image. These vectors from all the blocks are then joined together into one long list. This full list becomes the feature vector, a numeric representation of the entire image's shapes and contours.

Now that the image is summarized as a feature vector, the system needs a way to determine whether this vector represents a face (or a pedestrian, or any target object) or not. This is where the Support Vector Machine (SVM) comes in.

SVM is a machine learning classifier (Weston & Watkins, 1999). At its core, it is a decision-making algorithm trained on examples. During training, it is shown many examples of images with and without faces. For each image, it looks at the HOG feature vector and learns to find patterns that are characteristic of a face such as the general arrangement of edges around the eyes, nose, and mouth. It then figures out the best possible boundary or dividing line between "face" and "non-face" in the multi-dimensional space formed by these feature vectors (Chapelle & Vapnik, 1999). Once trained, the SVM can look at a new, unseen image, extract its HOG features, and determine on which side of the boundary this vector lies. If the feature vector is on the "face" side of the boundary, it classifies the image region as containing a face; otherwise, it's labeled as a non-face region.

The combination of HOG for describing the image's structural information and SVM for making the classification decision has proven to be very powerful and efficient. It was widely used in real-time systems before deep learning became mainstream because it didn't require enormous datasets or specialized hardware.

However, while SVM does a good job with the structured features provided by HOG, it's not adaptive to highly complex patterns like expressions, occlusions, or unusual poses. For that, more advanced models like Convolutional Neural Networks (CNNs) are preferred today. Nonetheless, the HOG + SVM pipeline laid the groundwork for understanding object structure and classification in modern vision systems (Wang & Deng, 2021).

Traditional face and object detection methods such as Viola-Jones, Histogram of Oriented Gradients (HOG) with Support Vector Machines (SVM), Principal Component Analysis (PCA), Linear Discriminant Analysis (LDA), and Local Binary Patterns (LBP) are rooted in classical mathematical and statistical frameworks. These methods played a foundational role in early computer vision systems and still form the basis for understanding the evolution of modern deep learning-based models (Viola & Jones, 2001; Dalal & Triggs, 2005; Martinez & Kak, 2001; Shan et al., 2009; Nefian & Hayes, 1998).

2.5 Viola-Jones: Haar Features and Cascaded Classifiers

The Viola-Jones face detection algorithm is based on Haar-like features and an integral image for fast computation. Mathematical formulation involves comparing rectangular regions of an image to identify edge- and texture-like patterns. The AdaBoost algorithm is employed to select and weigh the most relevant features, combining weak classifiers into a strong classifier (Viola & Jones, 2001).

The cascade classifier architecture uses a series of increasingly complex classifiers that reject non-face regions early and apply detailed analysis only to promising regions. This hierarchical approach ensures high computational efficiency (Viola & Jones, 2001).

Strengths:

- Fast, real-time performance due to integral image and cascade (Viola & Jones, 2001)
- Works well on frontal, upright faces in controlled lighting (Viola & Jones, 2001)
- Computationally efficient and easy to implement on low-resource devices (Viola & Jones, 2001)

Limitations:

- Fails under varying poses, occlusions, or illumination (Viola & Jones, 2001; Kortli et al., 2020)
- Requires extensive manual feature engineering (Viola & Jones, 2001)
- Limited accuracy on complex, real-world datasets (Kortli et al., 2020)

HOG + SVM: Edge Orientation Features with Linear Classification

The Histogram of Oriented Gradients (HOG) method extracts edge direction information from localized regions of an image. It computes gradients at each pixel, bins them into orientation histograms, and concatenates the results into a feature vector. This vector is then classified using a Support Vector Machine (SVM), which finds a decision boundary in high-dimensional space (Dalal & Triggs, 2005; Weston & Watkins, 1999).

PCA, LDA, ICA: Statistical Feature Extraction

These are appearance-based methods that reduce dimensionality and extract dominant features from facial images:

- PCA (Principal Component Analysis) identifies the axes (eigenfaces) that capture the most variance in the dataset. It reconstructs face images from a lower-dimensional subspace (Martinez & Kak, 2001).
- LDA (Linear Discriminant Analysis) maximizes the inter-class variance while minimizing intra-class variance, making it more suitable for classification than PCA (Delac et al., 2005).
- ICA (Independent Component Analysis) goes further to find statistically independent components, often interpreted as encoding localized facial features (e.g., eyes, mouth) (Shan et al., 2009).

Strengths:

- Effective for reducing data dimensionality (Martinez & Kak, 2001; Delac et al., 2005)
- PCA and LDA can be combined with classifiers like SVM or KNN (Shan et al., 2009; Delac et al., 2005)
- Easy to implement and compute (Martinez & Kak, 2001)

Limitations:

- Assumes linearity; fails to capture nonlinear patterns (Delac et al., 2005; Shan et al., 2009)
- Not robust to noise, occlusions, or misalignments (Shan et al., 2009)
- Requires preprocessing such as image alignment and normalization (Delac et al., 2005)

LBP, DCT, HMMs, and Bayesian Classifiers

- Local Binary Patterns (LBP) use pixel intensity differences in a neighborhood to encode texture information (Ojala et al., 2002). LBP features are then used with classifiers like SVM (Shan et al., 2009).

- Discrete Cosine Transform (DCT) compresses spatial information into frequency components and is effective in compact feature representation (Ahmed et al., 1974).
- Hidden Markov Models (HMMs) are used to model sequential patterns in facial expressions or temporal data (Nefian & Hayes, 1998).
- Bayesian classifiers rely on probabilistic decision-making using prior and likelihood distributions of classes (Bishop, 2006).

Strengths:

- LBP is computationally lightweight and effective in texture-based detection (Ojala et al., 2002)
- DCT is good for compression-based applications (e.g., MPEG) (Ahmed et al., 1974)
- HMMs model time-series data like facial movements (Nefian & Hayes, 1998)
- Bayesian methods are interpretable and handle uncertainty well (Bishop, 2006)

Limitations:

- LBP is sensitive to noise and scale (Ojala et al., 2002)
- DCT loses spatial localization (Ahmed et al., 1974)
- HMMs require extensive training data and are slow (Nefian & Hayes, 1998)
- Bayesian models require prior knowledge and are not always scalable (Bishop, 2006)

2.6 Deep Learning Models for Detection and Recognition

While traditional mathematical methods laid the groundwork for face and object detection systems, their performance in real-world, complex environments remains limited (Bakshi & Singhal, 2014; Kortli et al., 2020). These methods rely heavily on manual feature design, lack adaptability, and often fall short when

While traditional mathematical methods laid the groundwork for face and object detection systems, their performance in real-world, complex environments remains limited (Bakshi & Singhal, 2014; Kortli et al., 2020). These methods rely heavily on manual feature design, lack adaptability, and often fall short when confronted with challenges like pose variation, partial occlusion, and inconsistent lighting. These limitations ultimately led to the rise of deep learning-based approaches, which learn robust feature representations directly from data, outperforming classical methods across virtually all benchmarks (Wang & Deng, 2021).

The advent of deep learning has transformed the landscape of object and face detection, particularly in real-time surveillance applications **(Krizhevsky et al., 2012; Kortli et al., 2020)**. Convolutional Neural Networks (CNNs) and their derivatives such as **SSD** and **YOLO** have enabled significant improvements in accuracy, robustness to environmental variations, and processing speed **(Liu et al., 2016; Redmon et al., 2016)**. This chapter presents the foundational concepts, architectures, and mathematical underpinnings of these models.

2.6.1 Convolutional Neural Networks (CNN)

Convolutional Neural Networks (CNNs) are the cornerstone of modern computer vision **(LeCun et al., 1998)**. Unlike traditional machine learning models that rely on handcrafted features, CNNs automatically learn hierarchical features directly from image data **(Goodfellow et al., 2016)**. They consist of layers that mimic the visual cortex of the human brain, identifying low-level patterns like edges in early layers and progressing to complex patterns such as shapes or objects in deeper layers **(LeCun et al., 1998)**.

CNNs are composed of multiple learnable filters (kernels) that slide across the image to produce feature maps **(LeCun et al., 1998)**. These layers capture spatial hierarchies in the data, enabling the model to localize and recognize patterns effectively **(Krizhevsky et al., 2012)**. Due to their ability to learn robust features, CNNs are widely used in object detection, image classification **(LeCun et al., 1998; Dong et al., 2007)**, and face recognition tasks **(Wang & Deng, 2021)**.

Key Components:

- Local receptive fields (kernels) **(LeCun et al., 1998)**
- Weight sharing (reduces parameters) **(Goodfellow et al., 2016)**
- Deep stacked layers (hierarchical features) **(Krizhevsky et al., 2012)**

CNNs are used in this research to extract deep features for both detection and person identification (e.g., via **ResNet**, **FaceNet**) **(He et al., 2016; Schroff et al., 2015)**.

The field of face recognition has witnessed a transformative shift with the advent of deep learning **(Sun et al., 2014; Wang & Deng, 2021)**. Unlike traditional approaches that rely on hand-crafted features, deep learning models, particularly Convolutional Neural Networks (CNNs), can automatically learn hierarchical and discriminative features from large datasets **(Schroff et al., 2015)**. These models have drastically improved the accuracy, robustness, and scalability of face recognition systems, even under challenging conditions such as occlusion, variations in lighting, pose, and facial expressions **(Kortli et al., 2020; Wang & Deng, 2021)**.

This section discusses major contributions in the application of deep learning to face recognition, including CNN architectures, deep metric learning models like **FaceNet**, and pre-trained models such as **ResNet50** and **VGGFace** **(Schroff et al., 2015; He et al., 2016; Parkhi et al., 2015)**. It also highlights recent innovations like **Winograd CNN** aimed at reducing computational complexity while maintaining high recognition performance **(Liu et al., 2021)**.

Convolutional Neural Networks (CNN) for Feature Extraction

(Al-Saffar, Tao & Talab, 2017; Sharma et al., 2020)

CNNs have become the de facto architecture for face recognition due to their ability to automatically extract and learn robust feature representations from raw pixel data **(Al-Saffar et al., 2017; Sharma et al., 2020)**.

Key components of CNNs used in face recognition include:

- **Convolutional layers:** Detect local patterns such as edges, textures, and facial features **(LeCun et al., 1998)**.
- **Activation functions (e.g., ReLU):** Introduce non-linearity, enabling the model to learn complex functions **(Goodfellow et al., 2016)**.
- **Pooling layers:** Down sample feature maps to reduce spatial dimensions and computation **(Krizhevsky et al., 2012)**.
- **Fully connected layers:** Perform high-level reasoning for classification or embedding generation **(Schroff et al., 2015)**.

CNNs learn to extract deep facial features by training on large, labeled datasets **(Sun et al., 2014)**. Their ability to generalize makes them suitable for a wide range of applications such as identity verification, access control, and facial expression analysis **(Kortli et al., 2020)**.

Kaur P. and Sharma (2020) demonstrated the scalability of CNNs in handling large-scale face datasets, emphasizing the improvement in recognition accuracy as the network depth and data volume increase **(Kaur & Sharma, 2020)**. Al-Saffar et al. (2017) highlighted CNNs' superiority over traditional methods in managing complex, nonlinear image classification problems **(Al-Saffar et al., 2017)**.

FaceNet and Deep Metric Learning

(Schroff et al., 2015)

FaceNet is a groundbreaking face recognition system introduced by Schroff et al. that utilizes **deep metric learning** instead of conventional classification.

Key features:

- The model maps face images to a **128-dimensional embedding space** where Euclidean distances directly correspond to facial similarity.
- It is trained using the **triplet loss function**, which ensures that:
    - Distance (anchor, positive) < Distance (anchor, negative) + margin This enforces that faces of the same identity are closer than those of different identities.
- FaceNet can be used for:
    - **Face verification**: Determining whether two images are of the same person.
    - **Face clustering**: Grouping similar face images.
    - **Face identification**: Matching a face against a gallery of known faces.

FaceNet's architecture allows for real-time deployment and achieves **state-of-the-art accuracy** on benchmark datasets such as LFW (Labelled Faces in the Wild), making it a cornerstone of modern face recognition systems.

ResNet50 and VGGFace for Face Embedding and Recognition

(Liu et al., 2020; Zhang & Li, 2020)

Pre-trained deep CNN models such as **ResNet50** and **VGGFace** have proven highly effective for face recognition, especially when adapted using **transfer learning**.

- **ResNet50** (Residual Networks):
    - Incorporates **skip connections** to solve the vanishing gradient problem, allowing very deep networks to be trained effectively.

- Extracts **high-level, discriminative features** from facial images.
- Liu et al. (2020) utilized ResNet50 for face recognition under varying angles and lighting conditions, demonstrating its robustness and generalization ability.

- **VGGFace**:
  - Based on the VGG-16 architecture, it is trained on millions of face images.
  - Offers compact and efficient face descriptors (embeddings).
  - Commonly used as a feature extractor in face recognition pipelines due to its ease of integration and strong performance.

These models serve as strong **backbones for embedding generation**, particularly useful in systems where the downstream task (e.g., classification, clustering) is built on learned face vectors.

Winograd CNN for Computational Efficiency

(Liu et al., 2021)

The **Winograd CNN** is an optimization of conventional CNNs designed to **reduce the computational cost of convolution operations**, which are the most intensive part of the network.

Key highlights:

- Uses the **Winograd minimal filtering algorithm** to perform fast convolutions, reducing the number of multiplications required.
- Particularly effective for small kernel sizes (e.g., 3×3), which are common in modern CNN architectures.
- Maintains high recognition accuracy while significantly reducing memory and computational requirements.

Liu et al. (2021) implemented a 2D Winograd CNN in face recognition tasks and demonstrated that it offers **efficient inference** without sacrificing accuracy an important consideration for real-time or embedded systems.

Deep learning techniques have redefined face recognition by enabling:

- **Automatic, end-to-end learning** of features.
- **Higher accuracy** and **robustness** to variations.
- **Scalable architecture is** suitable for real-time and mobile applications.

While traditional methods offered valuable early contributions, deep learning has established itself as the dominant paradigm, particularly through models like FaceNet, ResNet50, and CNN-based optimizations like Winograd. These methods form the basis for further hybrid models integrating enhancement (e.g., ESRGAN), detection (YOLO), and temporal modeling (e.g., LSTM), as discussed in subsequent sections.

2.7 Convolution, Pooling, ReLU, and Softmax

CNN architecture typically follows a pattern involving **(LeCun et al., 1998; Goodfellow et al., 2016)**:

- **Convolution Layers:** Apply filters to the input image to extract spatial features such as edges, corners, and textures. Each filter responds to a specific pattern, creating a feature map **(LeCun et al., 1998; Krizhevsky et al., 2012)**.
- **ReLU (Rectified Linear Unit):** Introduces non-linearity to the network by converting negative activations to zero, allowing the model to learn complex mappings **(Nair & Hinton, 2010; Goodfellow et al., 2016)**.

- **Pooling Layers:** Reduce the spatial dimensions of feature maps, helping in computational efficiency and making the model invariant to small translations. Max pooling is the most common form, selecting the maximum value from a patch of the feature map **(Boureau et al., 2010; Krizhevsky et al., 2012)**.
- **Softmax Layer:** Typically used in classification tasks to convert the final output scores into probabilities, indicating the likelihood of each class **(Bishop, 2006; Goodfellow et al., 2016)**.

2.7.1 Feature Hierarchy and Filters

CNNs learn features in a hierarchical manner **(LeCun et al., 1998; Krizhevsky et al., 2012)**. The shallow layers focus on detecting basic edges and gradients, while deeper layers learn to recognize shapes, textures, and full objects **(Zeiler & Fergus, 2014)**. Each filter in a convolutional layer act as a detector for a specific pattern **(LeCun et al., 1998)**. During training, these filters are adjusted so that the network can effectively identify patterns relevant to the target task **(Goodfellow et al., 2016)**. This layered learning allows CNNs to generalize well across varied image data **(Krizhevsky et al., 2012)**.

CNNs learn increasingly abstract features across layers **(Zeiler & Fergus, 2014)**:

- **Lower layers** learn edges and textures **(LeCun et al., 1998)**.
- **Middle layers** learn motifs, corners, and contours **(Zeiler & Fergus, 2014)**.
- **Higher layers** learn object-specific features **(Krizhevsky et al., 2012)**.

This hierarchy makes CNNs highly effective in facial recognition, where subtle variations in eyes, noses, and mouths must be distinguished **(Sun et al., 2014; Wang & Deng, 2021)**.

2.8 Single Shot Multibox Detector (SSD)

The Single Shot Multibox Detector (SSD) is a deep learning object detection algorithm that detects objects in images using a single forward pass of the network, unlike region-based methods that perform two-stage processing **(Liu et al., 2016)**. SSD divides the input image into a grid and simultaneously predicts class probabilities and bounding box coordinates for multiple object classes at each grid location **(Liu et al., 2016)**.

SSD introduces multiple convolutional layers of decreasing size (feature maps) to detect objects of various scales **(Liu et al., 2016)**. It uses default boxes (also known as anchor boxes) of different aspect ratios and sizes to match ground truth objects **(Liu et al., 2016)**.

2.8.1 Anchor Boxes and Multiscale Detection

Anchor boxes are predefined bounding boxes of various sizes and aspect ratios assigned to each cell in the feature map **(Liu et al., 2016)**. These anchors act as initial guesses for object locations. The SSD model predicts how to adjust each anchor box to fit the actual object **(Ren et al., 2015; Liu et al., 2016)**.

By using feature maps of multiple scales (e.g., large for small objects, small for large objects), SSD ensures effective detection of both small and large objects **(Liu et al., 2016)**. This multiscale strategy improves accuracy, particularly in images with diverse object sizes **(Lin et al., 2017)**.

- Each location on feature maps predicts objects using anchor boxes of various aspect ratios **(Liu et al., 2016)**.
- Detection is performed on multiple scales (feature maps of varying resolutions) **(Liu et al., 2016; Lin et al., 2017)**.

Bounding box:

$$b = (cx, cy, w, h)$$

IoU (Intersection over Union) is used for box matching during training.

2.8.2 Loss Function: classification + localization

The SSD loss function is a combination of:

- Classification Loss: Measures the error between predicted and true class labels, typically using cross-entropy loss.
- Localization Loss: Measures the difference between the predicted bounding boxes and the ground truth using a smooth L1 loss (regression loss).

The total loss is a weighted sum of these two components, enabling the model to simultaneously learn where objects are and what they are.

The SSD loss function is a combination of classification and localization losses:

$$L = 1N(Lconf + \alpha Lloc)$$

- Lconf: Softmax loss for class prediction
- Lloc: Smooth L1 loss for bounding box regression
- α: Balancing weight

2.9 YOLOv5 to YOLOv12

YOLO **(You Only Look Once)** treats object detection as a single regression problem, making it extremely fast. YOLO family represents one of the most efficient real-time object detection models. Unlike SSD, which uses separate feature maps for different scales, YOLO divides the image into a grid and predicts bounding boxes and class probabilities directly from the grid cells.

- YOLOv5: Introduced PyTorch-based implementation with model variants (nano, small, medium, large, xlarge). It emphasizes modular design, ease of use, and deployment readiness.
- YOLOv6 and YOLOv7: Improved accuracy and introduced architectural optimizations (e.g., RepVGG, E-ELAN) and task-aware learning strategies.
- YOLOv8: Streamlined design, better anchor-free architecture, and support for instance segmentation.
- YOLOv12 (latest): Incorporates ViT-like transformer attention, sparse computation, dynamic anchors, and more advanced detection heads, enabling better generalization in complex scenes with minimal computational overhead.

2.9.1 Grid-cell Prediction and Bounding Boxes

YOLO models divide the image into an S×S grid, where each cell is responsible for predicting bounding boxes and class probabilities for objects whose center falls inside the cell. This allows real-time object detection by leveraging the full context of the image in a single pass.

Bounding box predictions include the box's center coordinates, width, height, and confidence score, indicating how likely the box contains an object and how accurate it is.

- The input image is divided into an S×S grid.
- Each grid cell predicts:
  - B bounding boxes
  - Objectness score
  - Class probabilities

$$\text{Final Score} = \text{Pobject} \cdot \text{IoUpred, truth} \cdot \text{Pclass}$$

The latest YOLOv12 integrates **Vision Transformers (ViT)**and **cross-scale feature attention** for enhanced performance in small or occluded object detection.

YOLO models are known for balancing speed and accuracy. Earlier versions prioritized speed, making them ideal for edge devices and real-time applications, but occasionally at the cost of detection precision.

With each version, YOLO has improved its accuracy without drastically compromising speed:

- YOLOv5 Nano: Extremely fast (~140 FPS) with lower accuracy.
- YOLOv7/8 Medium: Balanced for real-time applications (~30-60 FPS).
- YOLOv12: Optimized for maximum accuracy on complex scenes with transformer-based enhancements while preserving speed.

Trade-offs are carefully managed through model size, depth, feature scaling, and anchor selection.

2.9.2 Speed vs. Accuracy Trade-offs

Version	FPS	Precision	Use-case
YOLOv5	60+	Moderate	Lightweight edge devices
YOLOv8	50	High	Balanced performance
YOLOv12	45	Very High	Complex real-time applications

Table 2.1: Comparison of YOLO Versions

YOLO versions offer modularity small (nano) to large (x)allowing trade-offs between accuracy and speed.

2.10 Mathematical Formulations and Comparisons

CNN-based detectors use convolution operations as core computation: feature extraction relies on convolving filters over input data and applying non-linear activations. SSD formulates detection as a multi-object regression problem, using anchor boxes and joint loss functions for bounding box regression and classification. YOLO reformulates object detection as a single regression problem straight from image pixels to bounding box coordinates and class probabilities, enabling unparalleled speed.

Model	Key Formulation	Strengths	Limitations
CNN	$F(i,j) = \sum X \cdot K$ ReLU, pooling, softmax	Feature extraction, recognition	High computational load
SSD	$L = Lconf + Lloc$ multi-scale anchors	Fast, accurate for medium objects	Weaker on small object detection
YOLO	Grid-based prediction. $\text{confidence} = \text{obj} \times \text{IoU} \times \text{class}$	Fastest, real-time capability	Struggles with overlapping objects

Table 2.2: Comparative Summary of Deep Learning-Based Object Detection Models

Deep learning-based detection and recognition models such as CNN, SSD, and YOLO provide the foundation for accurate and real-time surveillance. This research integrates these models into a hybrid pipeline to balance detection accuracy, computational cost, and real-time performance crucial for campus security systems operating under resource and environment variability.

Histogram of Oriented Gradients (HOG) + Support Vector Machines (SVM) (Dalal & Triggs, 2005)

Dalal and Triggs introduced **HOG features**, a robust descriptor for object detection based on gradient orientation histograms. The process involves:

- **Gradient computation**: Capturing edge and texture information from grayscale images.

- **Cell and block normalization**: Aggregating local histograms across image patches to reduce sensitivity to illumination changes.
- **Feature vector formation**: The concatenated normalized histograms represent the final image descriptor.
- **SVM classification**: A linear or RBF-kernel SVM is trained to distinguish between face and non-face regions.

HOG + SVM is especially effective for **pedestrian and frontal face detection**, but it struggles with rotated or partially occluded faces.

PCA, LDA, and ICA for Face Feature Extraction

Statistical methods such as **Principal Component Analysis (PCA), Linear Discriminant Analysis (LDA)**, and **Independent Component Analysis (ICA)** were extensively used for face recognition before the deep learning era.

- **PCA (Belhumeur et al., 1997)**:
    - Also known as the **Eigenfaces method**.
    - Reduces dimensionality by projecting faces onto a lower-dimensional subspace that captures the most variance.
    - Good for unsupervised representation but lacks discriminative power for classification.

- **LDA (Martinez & Kak, 2001)**:
    - Also known as **Fisherfaces**.
    - Maximizes the **between-class variance** while minimizing **within-class variance**.

- Offers better classification accuracy than PCA, particularly in small sample settings.

- **ICA**:
  - Enhances upon PCA by capturing **higher-order statistical independence** rather than just decorrelation.
  - It can better handle complex lighting and facial expression variations.

These linear projection methods are computationally efficient but are limited by their inability to model non-linear variations.

LBP + SVM, DCT, HMMs, EBGM, and Bayesian Classifiers

Other traditional methods that contributed to early facial recognition systems include texture-based descriptors, probabilistic models, and statistical classifiers.

- **Local Binary Patterns (LBP) + SVM (Ahonen et al., 2006)**:
  - LBP encodes texture information by thresholding neighboring pixels around each center pixel.
  - Histograms of LBP code are used as feature descriptors.
  - When coupled with SVMs, LBP provides good recognition rates under uniform lighting but is sensitive to noise.
- **Discrete Cosine Transform (DCT)**:
  - Projects facial images into frequency domain.
  - Captures global appearance features and is used in compression and recognition tasks.
- **Hidden Markov Models (HMM) (Samaria & Harter, 1994)**:

    - Suitable for modeling **temporal sequences** and **spatial dependencies** in facial expressions or sequential data.
    - Effective for video-based or dynamic recognition tasks.
- **Elastic Bunch Graph Matching (EBGM) (Wiskott et al., 1997)**:
    - Uses Gabor filters at facial landmarks for feature extraction.
    - Graph structures allow for flexible matching of facial topologies.
- **Bayesian Classifiers (Friedman et al., 1997)**:
    - Estimate probability distributions of face and non-face classes.
    - Simple and interpretable but often outperformed by discriminative methods.

2.11 Automated Attendance Systems Using Face Recognition

Attendance monitoring has traditionally relied on manual methods such as roll calls, paper-based registers, or card-based systems. These approaches are **time-consuming**, **error-prone**, and susceptible to **proxy attendance** or manipulation. The advent of artificial intelligence and facial recognition technologies has enabled the development of **automated attendance systems** that improve accuracy, efficiency, and scalability in educational institutions.

This section reviews key research contributions that apply facial recognition to automate academic attendance both in physical classroom settings and remote learning environments. It also highlights the integration of **low-cost embedded hardware platforms**, such as Raspberry Pi, to implement cost-effective solutions suitable for real-time deployment in academic institutions.

Classroom and Academic Attendance Solutions

(Sajid et al., 2014; Patil & Shukla, 2014; Jayaswal & Agrawal, 2020)

Several researchers have proposed **face recognition-based systems** to automate the process of attendance in classrooms:

- **Sajid et al. (2014)** presented a **conceptual model** for automating attendance using facial recognition. Their work emphasized the limitations of traditional manual methods and proposed the integration of **camera-based systems** with real-time facial recognition software. This approach eliminates manual intervention and ensures a reliable attendance record.
- **Patil & Shukla (2014)** developed an embedded system utilizing a **classroom-mounted camera** to detect and recognize student faces in real time. Their method captured student faces at the beginning of each session and cross-referenced them against a pre-stored database to **log attendance automatically**. The system could work without requiring student participation and minimized disruption to class flow.
- **Jayaswal & Agrawal (2020)** enhanced this concept by proposing a more **scalable architecture** using **automated image capture** from IP cameras and integrating it with student management systems. They also incorporated face pre-processing steps such as **alignment, cropping, and normalization**, improving recognition accuracy in uncontrolled environments.

These approaches laid the groundwork for using computer vision and facial recognition in academic attendance, proving their effectiveness in reducing administrative workload while increasing data integrity.

Video Conferencing and Real-Time Academic Tools

(Jadhav et al., 2024)

The shift to **remote and hybrid learning environments**, particularly during the COVID-19 pandemic, accelerated the need for **face-based attendance systems** in online platforms.

- **Jadhav et al. (2024)** proposed a face recognition-based tool integrated with **video conferencing platforms** (e.g., Zoom, Google Meet). Their system:
  - ➢ Captures periodic screenshots of participant faces during the session.
  - ➢ Applies a **CNN-based facial recognition algorithm** to verify identity.
  - ➢ Logs attendance dynamically based on **face presence and consistency** across time intervals.

This approach addresses new challenges in online education such as **camera impersonation**, **multitasking**, or **false login credentials**. Their tool supports academic integrity by ensuring only enrolled students are marked present.

Real-time tools like this demonstrate the adaptability of face recognition systems to both physical and virtual learning environments, offering a **seamless user experience** without requiring manual input or secondary devices.

Raspberry Pi + Facial Recognition Implementations

(Subramani et al., 2021)

Cost and deployment scalability are often concerns in educational institutions, especially in developing regions. As a result, researchers have explored the use of **low-cost embedded platforms** like **Raspberry Pi** for automating attendance through facial recognition.

- **Subramani et al. (2021)** designed a **face recognition-based attendance system** using **Raspberry Pi** equipped with an HD camera module. Their contributions include:
  - ➢ A lightweight facial recognition algorithm based on **HOG + SVM or MobileNet** for embedded deployment.
  - ➢ Integration of **Wi-Fi and database connectivity**, allowing real-time attendance logging to cloud-based or local servers.

- An interface to display live student recognition feedback, providing transparency in attendance monitoring.

This system demonstrates how **edge computing devices** can reduce reliance on heavy server-side processing and offer an **energy-efficient, portable solution** that can be implemented even in classrooms without extensive IT infrastructure.

Furthermore, their model supports offline operation with batch synchronization, making it resilient to internet outages or power failures.

Automated attendance systems using face recognition:

- Address key inefficiencies in manual and card-based systems.
- Ensure higher **accuracy**, **security**, and **non-intrusive monitoring** of academic participation.
- Adapt flexibly to both **offline (in-class)** and **online (remote)** learning contexts.
- Leverage low-cost technologies (e.g., Raspberry Pi) for **scalable, real-world deployment** in educational institutions.

These systems not only reduce administrative burden but also enable **data-driven decision-making** by integrating with academic records and learning management systems (LMS). As face recognition technology matures, these systems will continue to evolve toward **real-time, context-aware**, and **privacy-preserving** attendance solutions forming an essential part of smart campus environments.

2.12 Object Detection Models in Surveillance

Object detection plays a pivotal role in intelligent video surveillance, serving as the foundational step for identifying, tracking, and analyzing persons and objects of interest. In the context of campus security, real-time detection must balance **speed, accuracy**, and **resource efficiency** to effectively identify students, staff, and anomalous behavior within dynamic environments. Traditional methods often struggle with occlusion, scale variation, and illumination changes. The emergence of deep learning-based object detection models especially the **YOLO (You Only Look Once)** family, **Single Shot Detector (SSD)**, **Faster R-CNN**, and hybrid architecture, has significantly improved performance in such complex conditions. These models are now widely used in surveillance applications due to their ability to **locate and classify multiple objects in real time**.

YOLO Family: Real-Time Detection with High Speed and Accuracy

(Daasan& Ishak, 2024; Chen et al., 2021)

The **YOLO (You Only Look Once)** architecture is one of the most prominent real-time object detectors, known for its **unified architecture** that performs both object localization and classification in a single pass.

- **YOLOv4**: Introduced CSPDarknet53 as its backbone and used optimizations like **Mish activation**, **SPP**, and **PANet** for multi-scale feature fusion. It demonstrated excellent performance in speed (FPS) and the mean average precision (mAP), making it suitable for real-time surveillance.
- **YOLOv8**: The latest iteration offers:
    - Enhanced backbone with **C2f modules** and decoupled head.
    - **Auto-labeling, multi-label classification**, and **pose estimation** support.
    - Superior performance across a wide range of tasks, including small and occluded face detection in surveillance videos.

- **YOLO-FaceV2**: Tailored specifically for face detection. It integrates **receptive field enhancement (RFE)** and **attention modules** to improve detection of **tiny, occluded, or low-resolution faces**, which are common in CCTV footage. Its compact architecture is ideal for **edge devices**.
- **E-YOLO (Efficient-YOLO)**: A fusion model that combines **EfficientNet** with YOLO's detection head to achieve a better trade-off between accuracy and computation. It is particularly effective when deployed on **low-power embedded systems** used in campus surveillance.

Daasan & Ishak (2024) demonstrated how integrating YOLOv8 with deep learning techniques improved person detection precision in academic environments. Chen et al. (2021) evaluated YOLOv4 against SSD and Faster R-CNN and concluded that YOLO provided superior **real-time accuracy**, particularly in multi-person surveillance tasks.

SSD, FSSD, and Faster R-CNN: Region-Based and One-Stage Detectors

(Weng et al., 2017)

While YOLO dominates in real-time scenarios, **Single Shot Detector (SSD)** and **Faster R-CNN** offer alternative frameworks for object detection:

- **SSD (Single Shot Detector)**:
    - ➢ Uses a **feature pyramid** to detect objects at different scales in a single forward pass.
    - ➢ Balances speed and accuracy, suitable for medium-complexity applications.
    - ➢ Works well for face/body detection in moderate-resolution video streams.
- **FSSD (Feature-Fused SSD)**:

- An enhancement of SSD that incorporates **multi-scale feature fusion** for improved performance on small objects.
- It integrates low-level fine-grained features with high-level semantic features.
- More robust under complex surveillance scenarios, such as partially occluded or distant individuals.

- **Faster R-CNN**:
  - A **two-stage detector**:
    - Stage 1: Region Proposal Network (RPN) suggests object-like regions.
    - Stage 2: A classifier and regressor operate on these proposals.
  - Although computationally intensive, Faster R-CNN offers **high precision** and is preferred for **offline video analysis** or tasks requiring **fine-grained classification** (e.g., weapon detection, suspicious object tracking).

Weng et al. (2017) conducted a comparative study and highlighted that Faster R-CNN excels in detection accuracy while SSD and YOLO are preferable in time-sensitive scenarios such as campus entrance monitoring or corridor surveillance.

Hybrid YOLO + CNN + ViT Approaches

(Sun et al., 2024)

Recent research explores **hybrid models** that combine the strengths of multiple deep learning architectures to overcome the limitations of individual models in surveillance applications.

- **YOLO + CNN + Vision Transformer (ViT)** hybrids leverage:
  - **YOLO's localization speed**,
  - **CNN's feature extraction power**, and

- **ViT's global attention mechanisms** for robust spatial understanding.

- **ViT (Vision Transformer)** models divide the image into patches and process them using transformer encoders, which capture **long-range dependencies** and **contextual awareness** better than CNNs alone.
- These hybrid systems excel in:
  - **Occlusion handling** (by understanding context),
  - **Multi-scale object detection**,
  - **Dynamic background adaptation** in surveillance footage.
- **Sun et al. (2024)** introduced a cascading model where:
  - YOLO performs initial region proposals,
  - CNN refines local features, and
  - ViT captures holistic scene-level relationships, achieving superior results in **low-light, crowded, and multi-camera campus environments**.

Such hybrid models are particularly promising for future AI-powered surveillance systems, including **real-time threat detection**, **behavior monitoring**, and **multi-object tracking** in academic institutions.

Object detection models are critical components of surveillance systems and determine the **accuracy, speed, and reliability** of subsequent modules like identification and behavior analysis.

The evolution of object detection methods reflects a trade-off:

Model	Detection Type	Best For	Speed	Accuracy
YOLOv4/v8	One-stage (real-	Real-time detection on campus	High	High

	time)			
SSD / FSSD	One-stage	Moderate complexity, small object detection	Medium	Moderate
Faster R-CNN	Two-stage	Offline analysis, precision-critical tasks	Low	Very High
Hybrid YOLO-CNN-ViT	Cascaded	Context-aware detection, occlusions	Medium	Very High

Table 2.3: Evolution Of Object Detection Methods

2.13 Image and Video Enhancement for Surveillance

In surveillance systems, especially those deployed in **uncontrolled environments** like university campuses, the quality of captured footage plays a critical role in downstream tasks such as **face recognition**, **object detection**, and **behavior analysis**. Factors such as **low resolution**, **poor lighting**, **motion blur**, **occlusions**, and **compression artifacts** significantly degrade the effectiveness of detection and identification models.

To address these challenges, researchers have developed **image and video enhancement techniques** that improve the **visual clarity** and **feature integrity** of surveillance frames. This section reviews key methods including **Enhanced Super-Resolution GAN (ESRGAN)**, **wavelet-transformed image processing**, and **illumination invariant enhancement**, which are instrumental in improving recognition accuracy in real-time video surveillance applications.

Enhanced Super-Resolution GAN (ESRGAN)

(Wang et al., 2019)

ESRGAN is a **Generative Adversarial Network (GAN)** designed to perform **super-resolution** by converting low-resolution (LR) images into high-resolution (HR) images while preserving perceptual quality and structural detail.

Key components of ESRGAN:

- **Generator Network**: Uses residual-in-residual dense blocks (RRDBs) to progressively refine image features.
- **Discriminator Network**: Employs relativistic average GAN (RaGAN) loss to focus on texture-level realism.
- **Perceptual Loss**: Derived from a pre-trained VGG network, it guides the model to enhance details that are semantically meaningful (e.g., facial features).

Advantages of surveillance:

- Restores fine facial textures and contours lost due to camera distance, compression, or poor lighting.
- Enhances **tiny faces** and **blurred objects**, improving the performance of downstream detection (YOLO, SSD) and recognition (FaceNet, SVM) models.
- Operates effectively in **low-resource setups** when optimized for GPU acceleration, making it viable for near real-time applications.

In the hybrid AI surveillance system, ESRGAN can be deployed as a **preprocessing module** that refines raw CCTV footage, thereby **boosting detection accuracy and identity verification** under suboptimal capture conditions.

Wavelet-Transformed Image Methods

(Guo et al., 2019)

Wavelet transformation is a classical signal processing technique that decomposes an image into **multiple frequency sub bands**, capturing both **coarse structure** and **fine details**.

Guo et al. (2019) applied wavelet-based methods in combination with **Support Vector Machines (SVM)** for face recognition in low-quality surveillance frames. Their approach involved:

- Decomposing facial images using **Discrete Wavelet Transform (DWT)**.
- Extracting coefficients from **high-frequency bands** (edges, contours) and **low-frequency bands** (texture, lighting).
- Feeding these coefficients as features into a classification model (e.g., SVM, PCA-LDA hybrid).

Relevance to surveillance:

- Wavelet features are robust to **noise**, **blur**, and **illumination changes**.
- Suitable for **compressed CCTV streams** and **frame-by-frame face detection**.
- Can be fused with deep learning models to **improve feature diversity and robustness**.

Illumination Invariant Techniques

(Li et al., 2021)

Variations in lighting conditions such as backlighting, shadows, and night-time capture pose significant challenges to surveillance systems. To overcome these, researchers have proposed **illumination invariant feature extraction techniques**, aimed at preserving consistent visual features across diverse lighting environments.

Li et al. (2021) proposed a method that integrates:

- **Retinex-based preprocessing**: Enhances image contrast and dynamic range by simulating human visual perception.
- **Color space normalization**: Converts RGB images to illumination-independent spaces (e.g., HSV, YCbCr).
- **Histogram equalization and contrast stretching**: Used to normalize pixel intensity distributions.

Impact on surveillance:

- Enhance facial details in **poorly lit indoor** or **night-time outdoor** settings.
- Improves object detection models' robustness by reducing false negatives due to underexposed regions.
- Particularly useful in **dormitory corridors, parking areas, or classrooms during power-saving modes** where ambient lighting is low.

These techniques are essential to ensure consistent feature extraction and identification accuracy throughout the day and across varying environmental conditions.

Image and video enhancement techniques are essential components in AI-powered surveillance systems. They **prepare raw input frames** for further processing by improving quality, consistency, and visual clarity.

Below is a comparative overview of their applications:

Technique	Target Problem	Approach	Application in Surveillance
ESRGAN	Low-resolution footage	GAN-based super-resolution	Enhances facial/textural detail in CCTV
Wavelet Transform	Compression noise, blur	Multi-scale frequency analysis	Robust feature extraction for SVM/CNN
Illumination Invariance	Varying lighting conditions	Retinex, histogram equalization	Improves consistency in face/object detection

Table 2.4: Comparative Overview of their Applications

Modern surveillance systems often suffer from low-quality video frames due to compression, bandwidth constraints, low lighting, or camera limitations. Enhancing the resolution of such frames is critical for downstream tasks like face recognition, object detection, and behavior analysis. **Super-resolution (SR)** algorithms, especially those based on deep learning, have shown remarkable performance in improving visual quality. Among them, **Enhanced Super-Resolution Generative Adversarial Network (ESRGAN)** is widely adopted due to its perceptual quality and reconstruction accuracy.

2.14 Role in Frame Clarity and Downstream Performance

Super-resolution, especially via ESRGAN, plays a pivotal role in enhancing:

- **Facial features** for identification (e.g., eye shape, skin texture).
- **Edge definition** for object detection models (YOLO, SSD).
- **Motion clarity** for behavior analysis models (RAFT, LSTM).

Without SR:

- Face recognizers might fail to generate embeddings.
- Detectors misclassify blurry regions.
- Motion patterns are lost due to pixel ambiguity.

With ESRGAN:

- Input images are sampled with preserved texture and contrast.
- Downstream AI models exhibit improved accuracy, particularly in low-light or distant camera conditions.

2.15 Equations for GAN Loss and Network Optimization

To train **ESRGAN**, the model needs guidance in the form of a **loss function**, a formula that tells it how far it is from generating realistic images **(Wang et al., 2019)**.

The breakdown of the three major loss components that guide **ESRGAN's learning (Wang et al., 2019)**:

1. Content Loss (Pixel Difference)

This measures how different the generated image is from the real image on a pixel level. It is often based on **L1 norm (absolute differences) (Ledig et al., 2017; Wang et al., 2019)**.

Intuition:

"How close is my image to the real one in terms of color and intensity for each pixel?"

2. Perceptual Loss (Feature-level Difference)

Instead of focusing on pixels, this loss compares how similar the features of the image are. These features are extracted from a **pre-trained network (e.g., VGG-19) (Johnson et al., 2016; Simonyan & Zisserman, 2015)**.

Intuition:

"Does my generated image look realistic to a human, with proper textures and patterns?"

This is crucial for surveillance, where slight detail differences can determine whether a face is recognized or not **(Wang et al., 2019; Kortli et al., 2020)**.

3. Adversarial Loss (From Discriminator)

This comes from the discriminator's judgment. The generator improves if it can fool the discriminator **(Goodfellow et al., 2014)**.

ESRGAN uses a **relativistic discriminator**, which evaluates the realism of images relative to one another (i.e., whether one image is more realistic than another) **(Jolicoeur-Martineau, 2019; Wang et al., 2019)**.

Intuition:

"Is my fake image getting more convincing than the real ones over time?"

2.16 Motion Analysis and Behavior Detection

In intelligent video surveillance systems, particularly those deployed in dynamic environments such as university campuses, the analysis of **motion patterns** and **behavioral cues** is essential for identifying abnormal activities (e.g., violence, trespassing, or loitering). While facial recognition and object detection address the **"who"** and **"what"**, behavior analysis helps interpret the **"how"** and **"why"**, offering deeper contextual insights for real-time threat assessment and crowd monitoring.

Modern behavior detection systems rely on **temporal modeling** capturing not only static frame information but also how objects and individuals move over time. Techniques such as **dense optical flow**, **recurrent neural networks (RNNs)**, and **two-stream architecture** have been widely adopted to model motion, detect anomalies, and recognize violent behavior. This section elaborates on four key approaches: RAFT for optical flow, LSTM-based sequence modeling, two-stream SepConvLSTM networks, and CNN-RNN hybrid architectures.

Real-time surveillance systems require not only the identification of individuals and objects but also the understanding of how these entities move and behave over time. Motion analysis and temporal pattern recognition are crucial for interpreting activities, identifying anomalies, and classifying behavior in video streams. This chapter elaborates on RAFT and LSTM two powerful tools used in this study for optical flow computation and sequential behavior modeling, respectively.

RAFT for Dense Optical Flow

(Teed & Deng, 2020)

RAFT (Recurrent All-Pairs Field Transforms) represents a breakthrough in **dense optical flow estimation**, a task that involves computing the pixel-wise motion between video frames. Unlike sparse optical flow that tracks only selected points, dense flow analyzes the entire image field crucial for tracking multiple moving subjects simultaneously.

Key innovations of RAFT:

- Constructs a **correlation volume** by computing similarity scores between all pixel pairs of two frames.
- Uses a **recurrent GRU-based update operator** to refine the flow estimate over multiple iterations.
- Provides **sub-pixel accuracy** and works well under occlusion, motion blur, and lighting variations.

Relevance to surveillance:

- Captures fine-grained motion patterns, which are critical in understanding behavioral anomalies.
- Effective in crowded scenes such as hallways or cafeterias.
- Acts as a motion descriptor input to temporal models like LSTM or ConvLSTM for activity classification.

LSTM and ConvLSTM for Temporal Modeling

(Hochreiter &Schmidhuber, 1997; Sudhakaran & Lanz, 2017)

Long Short-Term Memory (LSTM) networks are a variant of recurrent neural networks designed to **learn temporal dependencies** in sequential data. They are particularly effective for processing video sequences where understanding the **order and evolution** of actions is essential.

- **Standard LSTM** captures temporal relationships using memory cells and gating mechanisms (input, forget, and output gates), making it suitable for sequential motion features or optical flow vectors.
- **Convolutional LSTM (ConvLSTM)** extends LSTM by replacing matrix multiplications with **convolutions**, allowing it to retain **spatial structure** in addition to temporal modeling.

Applications in behavior detection:

- Sudhakaran & Lanz (2017) used ConvLSTM for **violence detection**, showing that combining frame differencing with temporal modeling can effectively detect sudden, aggressive motions.
- LSTMs can classify behaviors such as walking, standing, running, or fighting based on the motion sequence over time.

In surveillance, these models help detect behaviors that evolve over a few seconds and are difficult to capture through single-frame analysis.

Two-Stream SepConvLSTM Networks

(Islam et al., 2021)

To improve the granularity of motion understanding, **Islam et al. (2021)** proposed a **two-stream SepConvLSTM network**, designed specifically for behavior analysis in video surveillance.

Architecture components:

- **Stream 1 (Motion stream)**: Processes frame differences, capturing immediate temporal variations.
- **Stream 2 (Background-suppressed stream)**: Focuses on moving foreground objects by eliminating static backgrounds using subtraction or semantic segmentation.
- **SepConvLSTM layers**: Combine **separable convolution** and **temporal memory** to model spatial-temporal dynamics with fewer parameters and better efficiency.

Advantages:

- Captures **short-term actions** (e.g., sudden motion bursts) and **long-term behaviors** (e.g., loitering).

- Works well on challenging datasets like **RWF-2000** with real-world surveillance footage.
- Effective in resource-constrained edge environments due to its lightweight architecture.

This architecture is highly applicable to university surveillance scenarios where behaviors like crowding, vandalism, or conflict need to be detected in real-time.

CNN-RNN Hybrids for Violence Detection

(Traoré & Akhloufi, 2024; Contardo et al., 2023)

Hybrid architecture that combines **Convolutional Neural Networks (CNNs)** for spatial feature extraction with **Recurrent Neural Networks (RNNs)** like LSTM or GRU for temporal modeling have emerged as powerful tools in behavior detection.

- **Traoré & Akhloufi (2024)** proposed a CNN-RNN framework that:
  - Uses CNN layers to extract **visual features** from each frame (e.g., facial expressions, body posture).
  - Feeds sequences of these features into LSTM units to **model temporal transitions**.
  - Achieved **state-of-the-art results** in detecting aggressive and violent actions in video surveillance.
- **Contardo et al. (2023)** presented a **MobileNetV2 + ConvLSTM** model that balances accuracy and computational efficiency, making it suitable for **deployment on edge devices**. Their model was trained on benchmark datasets and reached an accuracy of **94.1%**, showing promise for **real-time violence detection**.

Advantages:

- Able to generalize well across different camera angles and scenes.

- Efficient enough for deployment in live CCTV systems across classrooms, corridors, or hostel premises.
- Bridges the gap between per-frame feature learning (CNN) and sequential motion analysis (RNN).

Motion analysis and behavior detection are essential for proactive surveillance. By combining dense motion estimation (RAFT), spatiotemporal modeling (LSTM/ConvLSTM), and hybrid CNN-RNN architectures, surveillance systems can evolve from simple tracking tools to **context-aware, behavior-sensitive platforms**.

2.16.1 RAFT (Recurrent All-Pairs Field Transforms)

RAFT is a state-of-the-art deep learning model for computing dense optical flow, proposed by Teed and Deng (2020). It significantly improves the estimation of motion between consecutive video frames, even in complex scenes. It is a cutting-edge deep learning model used to estimate dense optical flow between two consecutive video frames. Optical flow refers to the pattern of apparent motion of objects in a scene caused by the relative movement between the observer (camera) and the scene.

RAFT was introduced by Teed and Deng (2020) and stands out because of its:

- Accuracy in tracking pixel-level motion,
- Use of all-pairs correlations, and
- It is an ability to iteratively refine the flow field using recurrent units.

It forms the foundation of motion analysis in real-time video surveillance, especially when tracking the movements of individuals or identifying unusual activity (e.g., running, loitering, trespassing).

2.16.2 Optical Flow and Dense Motion Field Computation

In traditional optical flow methods like Farneback or Lucas-Kanade, only sparse or approximate flow estimates are obtained. In contrast, RAFT computes a dense motion field, meaning it calculates how every pixel in the first frame moves to its new position in the second frame.

1. Feature Extraction:
    - Two consecutive frames are passed through a convolutional neural network (CNN) to extract deep feature maps.
2. All-Pairs Correlation:
    - RAFT computes correlations between every pixel in the first image and every pixel in the second, creating a rich correlation volume that captures pixel-level similarities.
3. Recurrent Refinement:
    - A recurrent GRU-based update block then iteratively improves the flow estimation using the correlation volume, allowing precise and stable motion tracking.

This iterative refinement enables RAFT to capture fine details of movement, even in complex scenes with occlusion, lighting changes, or overlapping objects.

2.16.3 Role in Trajectory Tracking

RAFT is especially useful in surveillance settings because it generates coherent motion vectors that can be chained together over time to form trajectories.

These trajectories:

- Help in tracking individual persons across frames,

- Enable detection of motion patterns (e.g., running in a restricted area, standing unusually long in one location),
- Feed into higher-level modules like behavior classification models (e.g., LSTM networks).

In the hybrid system, RAFT serves as the motion extractor, giving temporal models like LSTM the raw movement data they need to understand behavior.

- **Dense trajectories** are generated by chaining pixel-wise motion vectors over frames.
- Helps track human movement paths (e.g., walking, running, loitering) across camera views.
- Used in this research to derive **motion features** for behavior recognition via LSTM.

RAFT is especially useful in surveillance settings because it generates coherent motion vectors that can be chained together over time to form trajectories.

These trajectories:

- Help in tracking individual persons across frames,
- Enable detection of motion patterns (e.g., running in a restricted area, standing unusually long in one location),
- Feed into higher-level modules like behavior classification models (e.g., LSTM networks).

In the hybrid system, RAFT serves as the motion extractor, giving temporal models like LSTM the raw movement data they need to understand behavior.

- **Dense trajectories** are generated by chaining pixel-wise motion vectors over frames.
- Helps track human movement paths (e.g., walking, running, loitering) across camera views.
- Used in this research to derive **motion features** for behavior recognition via LSTM.

2.17 Long Short-Term Memory (LSTM)

LSTM, or Long Short-Term Memory, is a type of Recurrent Neural Network (RNN) designed to learn from sequential data. It was introduced by Hochreiter and Schmidhuber (1997) to solve the vanishing gradient problem in standard RNNs.

LSTMs are widely used in speech recognition, machine translation, and now increasingly in video analysis and behavior classification, where patterns occur over time.

2.17.1 Gates, Memory Cells, Temporal Sequence Learning

At the heart of LSTM is the memory cell, which allows it to retain information across long time intervals. This is made possible by three special mechanisms called gates:

1. Forget Gate: Decides what information from the previous state to forget.
2. Input Gate: Decides what new information to add to the memory.
3. Output Gate: Controls what information to output from the cell.

These gates allow LSTM to selectively remember or forget information over time, making it ideal for modeling behaviors that unfold gradually, such as:

- Walking vs. running,
- Standing still vs. loitering,
- Aggressive movements.

Each input to the LSTM (in this context, motion features from RAFT) updates the hidden state and memory, allowing the network to build an internal representation of how behavior evolves over time.

2.18 Behavior Classification from Motion Features

The final goal is to classify human behavior based on the movement patterns extracted by RAFT and modeled by LSTM.

The pipeline works as follows:

1. Frame Sequence Input: A short video segment is broken into consecutive frames.

2. Motion Extraction: RAFT computes motion vectors between frames.
3. Temporal Modeling: These vectors are fed into an LSTM which processes the sequence.
4. Prediction: The LSTM outputs a classification label such as:
    - Normally walking,
    - Loitering,
    - Trespassing,
    - Running,
    - Fighting.

This setup forms the behavioral intelligence layer in the surveillance system. Since the classification is based on movement over time, it goes beyond static snapshots and offers context-aware analysis, essential for identifying threats before they escalate.

Workflow:

1. **Input:** RAFT-generated optical flow vectors per frame
2. **Temporal Aggregation**: Sequences of motion features collected over time windows
3. **LSTM**: Trained to learn the dynamics of normal vs abnormal motion
4. **Classifier**: Final dense layer with softmax activation for behavior labels

Output classes might include:

- Normal behavior: walking, sitting, entering room
- Suspicious behavior: loitering, fleeing, aggressive motion

2.19 Mathematical Modeling of Time Series and Flow

While we avoid heavy formulas here, conceptually:

- Motion field: RAFT provides a vector field (u, v), where each vector indicates how a pixel moved from one frame to the next.
- Time series: These vector fields are treated as sequences: M1,M2,...,MTM_1, M_2, ..., M_T across T frames.
- Sequence learning: LSTM models this time series and learns transitions like "still → motion → still" to identify loitering, or "fast → slow → stop" for tracking suspicious pauses.

By combining spatial motion extraction (RAFT) and temporal behavior modeling (LSTM), the system gains the ability to reason about actions, not just appearances.

2.20 Person Re-Identification (Re-ID) Techniques

Person Re-Identification (Re-ID) refers to the task of recognizing and matching individuals across multiple non-overlapping camera views in a surveillance network. Unlike face recognition, which focuses on facial features, Re-ID uses **full-body appearance**, **clothing**, **gait**, and **contextual cues** to track individuals when facial visibility is low or compromised.

In the context of **university campus surveillance**, Re-ID is essential for:

- Tracking students and visitors across departments and buildings,
- Monitoring unusual movements (e.g., loitering, trespassing),
- Strengthening multi-camera behavior analysis and identity continuity.

This section explores key developments in deep learning-based Re-ID systems, focusing on **deep-person networks**, **loss function engineering**, **attention mechanisms**, and **dataset benchmarking**.

In real-time surveillance systems, accurate identification of individuals is critical for maintaining campus security. Traditional face recognition systems rely on handcrafted features which often fail under variations in lighting, pose, and occlusion. Deep learning-based face embedding models like **FaceNet,** when combined with **Deep SVM classifiers**, offer robust solutions by transforming facial images into compact, discriminative feature vectors.

Deep-Person and Part-Based CNNs (PCB)

(Xiang Bai et al., 2017)

Deep-Person and **Part-Based Convolutional Baseline (PCB)** models introduced a novel approach to person Re-ID by combining **global and part-based features**.

- **Deep-Person**: Utilizes a three-branch architecture:
    - **Global branch**: Captures full-body features.
    - **Local branch**: Extracts part-level features from vertical body segments.
    - **LSTM branch**: Models contextual dependencies across parts.
- **PCB (Part-based CNN)**:
    - Splits feature maps into **horizontal stripes** (parts).
    - Extracts feature from each part independently.
    - Train a separate classifier for each part to improve discriminative learning.

Advantages in campus environments:

- Effective in **crowded or occluded scenes**, where full-body features may be partially visible.
- Captures **pose-invariant representations**, crucial for tracking individuals from different angles.

- Performs well under **clothing variations** and illumination shifts common in real-world footage.

These models form a strong foundation for accurate Re-ID and are commonly used as **baselines in Re-ID benchmarks**.

Triplet and Quadruplet Loss Strategies

(Hermans et al., 2017; Chen et al., 2017)

Metric learning plays a pivotal role in Re-ID by training models to embed visually similar instances closer and dissimilar ones farther in the feature space.

- **Triplet Loss** (Hermans et al., 2017):
    - Trains on anchor-positive-negative triplets.
    - Ensures:

      `Distance (anchor, positive) + margin < Distance (anchor, negative)`
    - Encourages **discriminative feature embeddings**.
- **Quadruplet Loss** (Chen et al., 2017):
    - Adds an additional negative sample to the triplet loss formulation.
    - Improves **intra-class compactness** and **inter-class separability**.
    - Better suited for scenarios with **high appearance variability**.

Impact on surveillance:

- Helps the model **learn similar relationships** between images of the same person under different cameras or conditions.
- Particularly useful in campus environments with **frequent outfit changes** or **camera angle shifts**.

These loss functions have become standard in **Re-ID architecture**, often used alongside classification losses for robust training.

Attention and Multi-Granular Networks

(Hu et al., 2018; Wang et al., 2018)

Attention mechanisms have been widely adopted to enable Re-ID models to **focus on discriminative parts** of the image while ignoring irrelevant background clutter.

- **Squeeze-and-Excitation (SE) Networks** (Hu et al., 2018):
  - Dynamically re-calibrate channel-wise feature responses.
  - Helps the model learn **what features are important**, improving representational power.
- **Multi-Granular Networks (MGN)** (Wang et al., 2018):
  - Simultaneously learn **global and local features** from different granularities.
  - Combines high-level semantic understanding with fine-grained local cues.
  - Highly effective in **multi-camera environments** and for **crowd Re-ID**.

Benefits in surveillance systems:

- Enhances Re-ID accuracy in **cluttered scenes**, e.g., cafeterias or libraries.
- Improves model robustness to **partial occlusion**, such as backpacks or head coverings.
- Useful in edge cases where individuals share **similar clothing or build**.

Attention-based models significantly improve **feature selectivity**, making them ideal for high-traffic campus environments with variable visual data.

Dataset Challenges and Benchmarks

(Karanam et al., 2016)

The development and evaluation of Re-ID systems heavily depend on **benchmark datasets**. However, most datasets present **limitations** in terms of context, realism, and diversity when applied to **campus-specific surveillance**.

- **Market-1501**:
  - It contains over 32,000 images of 1,501 identities.
  - Captured from six cameras on a university campus.
  - Provides a solid baseline but is often criticized for limited occlusion and illumination variation.
- **DukeMTMC-ReID**:
  - Derived from the DukeMTMC multi-camera surveillance project.
  - Features more diverse environmental conditions and camera viewpoints.
  - Ideal for evaluating **multi-camera Re-ID performance**.

Challenges:

- Lack of **diverse campus-specific datasets** (e.g., classrooms, dormitories, labs).
- Need for **temporal continuity** and **behavior labels** in Re-ID data.
- Bias toward **controlled lighting** and **limited crowd density** in existing datasets.

Karanam et al. (2016) proposed a unified framework for evaluating Re-ID models using standard protocols (Rank-1 accuracy, mAP), emphasizing the need for **realistic, task-specific datasets**.

Person Re-Identification is a key enabler for tracking individuals across multiple surveillance zones. Deep learning has advanced this field through part-aware models, metric learning, attention mechanisms, and structured benchmarks.

2.20.1FaceNet

FaceNet (Schroff et al., 2015) is a deep learning model that learns a mapping from facial images to a compact **128-dimensional embedding space**. In this space, Euclidean distances directly correspond to facial similarity.

FaceNet is a deep convolutional neural network architecture introduced by Schroff et al. in 2015, designed specifically for face recognition, verification, and clustering. Unlike traditional classification models, FaceNet does not classify faces directly into identity labels. Instead, it maps each face image to a 128-dimensional embedding space, where geometric proximity represents face similarity.

How it Works:

FaceNet processes face images through a deep CNN and outputs a compact vector representation (embedding) for each face. These embeddings are used to compare faces rather than raw images. The key idea is that the faces of the same person lie close together in this embedding space, while the faces of different individuals are far apart.

2.20.2 Triplet Loss and Face Embedding Generation

Triplet Loss:

FaceNet uses a special training strategy called triplet loss, which is crucial for learning effective embeddings. The network is trained using triplets of images:

1. Anchor: A reference image of a person.
2. Positive: Another image of the same person.
3. Negative: An image of a different person.

The goal is to ensure that the distance between the anchor and positive is smaller than the distance between the anchor and negative, by a margin α. This encourages embeddings of the same identity to cluster together while pushing apart different identities.

Face Embedding:

The embedding generated by FaceNet is a numerical vector (typically 128-dimensions) that uniquely represents the facial characteristics of the individual, independent of pose, lighting, or background. These embeddings are later compared using similarity metrics like cosine similarity or Euclidean distance to match identities.

Triplet Loss Function:

$$L = \sum i = 1N[\| f(xiA) - f(xiP) \| 22 - \| f(xiA) - f(xiN) \| 22 + \alpha] +$$

Where:

- f(x): Embedding function
- α: Margin to prevent overlap
- $[z]+= \max(z, 0)$

Embedding Properties:

- Euclidean distances between same-person embeddings are minimized.
- Distances between different-person embeddings are maximized.

2.21 Deep Support Vector Machine (Deep SVM)

After embeddings are extracted via FaceNet, classification is performed using a **Deep Support Vector Machine (SVM).** SVMs are powerful margin-based classifiers suitable for small-sample, high-dimensional feature spaces.

Definition:

A Support Vector Machine (SVM) is a powerful machine learning classifier that finds the optimal hyperplane separating different classes in a dataset. A Deep SVM extends this idea by using features extracted from deep learning models (like FaceNet embeddings) rather than raw input features.

By combining the deep, feature extraction capabilities of CNNs with the discriminative power of SVMs, Deep SVMs are particularly effective in identity recognition and classification tasks.

2.21.1 Kernel-Based Classification

In many real-world problems, face embeddings may not be linearly separable. To overcome this, SVMs use kernel functions to transform the input feature space into a higher-dimensional space where a linear separation is possible.

Common kernel functions include:

- Linear kernel: Good for linearly separable data.
- Polynomial kernel: Captures nonlinear relations.
- Radial Basis Function (RBF) kernel: Most used for face embeddings due to its flexibility.

The kernel trick allows SVMs to handle complex decision boundaries without explicitly computing the higher-dimensional mappings.

SVM defines a hyperplane to separate classes. For nonlinear separation, kernel functions are used:

$$K(xi, xj) = \phi(xi)T\phi(xj)$$

Common kernels:

- **Linear**: $K(xi, xj) = xiTxj$
- **RBF**: $K(xi, xj) = \exp(-\gamma \parallel xi - xj \parallel 2)$
- **Polynomial**:$K(xi, xj) = (xiTxj + c)d$

SVM optimization objective:

$$\min w, b12 \parallel w \parallel 2 + C\sum i = 1N\xi i \text{ subject to } yi(wT\phi(xi) + b) \geq 1 - \xi i$$

Where:

- C: Regularization parameter
- ξi: Slack variables

2.21.2 Multi-Class Decision Boundaries

While basic SVMs are binary classifiers, real-world face recognition involves multiple identities. This requires multi-class SVMs, which are built using strategies like:

- One-vs-One: Train a binary classifier for every pair of classes.
- One-vs-Rest: Train one classifier per class, treating all other classes as a single negative class.

In the context of Deep SVM, each class (person) is represented by its own region in the embedding space. The SVM constructs boundaries between these regions, ensuring correct classification.

- For multi-class identification, **One-vs-Rest (OvR)** or**One-vs-One (OvO)** strategies are used.
- In this research, the SVM model outputs an identity label from the university's known identity database.

2.22 Cosine Similarity, FRR, FAR, and Identity Matching

Cosine similarity is a metric used to measure the angle between two vectors in an embedding space. For two face embeddings, it quantifies how "directionally similar" they are.

A cosine similarity of:

- 1 → perfect match (same person),

- 0 → orthogonal vectors (different persons),
- -1 → completely opposite.

In face recognition, higher cosine similarity implies closer identity.

False Rejection Rate (FRR):

FRR refers to the percentage of genuine users who are incorrectly rejected by the system. This happens when the similarity between the anchor and positive is not high enough to be accepted as the same person.

FRR = False Rejections / Total Genuine Attempts

High FRR reduces usability and user satisfaction.

False Acceptance Rate (FAR):

FAR is the percentage of imposters who are incorrectly accepted as genuine users. This happens when the similarity between the anchor and negative is mistakenly high.

FAR = False Acceptances / Total Imposter Attempts

A high FAR is a security risk.

Identity Matching:

To verify identity:

- The system computes the embedding of the new (query) image.
- It compares it with the stored embeddings using cosine similarity or Euclidean distance.
- If the similarity is above a threshold, it is a match; else, it is a non-match.

The threshold value is crucial:

- A lower threshold reduces FRR but increases FAR,
- A higher threshold reduces FAR but may increase FRR.

Balancing FAR and FRR is key to designing secure and usable face recognition systems.

2.23 Hybrid AI Models and Architectures

While deep learning models have achieved remarkable success in computer vision tasks, real-world deployment, especially in surveillance systems, often demands **hybrid architectures** that combine the strengths of multiple machine learning techniques. These hybrid models are particularly effective when dealing with **limited hardware**, **data imbalance**, **real-time constraints**, or the need for **interpretability** and **low-latency decision-making**.

In campus surveillance systems, hybrid architecture offers an efficient and scalable approach to **identity recognition**, **behavior monitoring**, and **system optimization**, especially when working across diverse conditions such as lighting variations, occlusion, or low-resolution frames. This section reviews significant contributions in the development of hybrid models, including **CNN-SVM integrations**, **deep identity embeddings**, and **lightweight embedded systems** with MLP and ensemble classifiers.

CNN + SVM Integration for Identity Recognition

(Accattoli et al., 2020)

The integration of **Convolutional Neural Networks (CNNs)** with **Support Vector Machines (SVMs)** has been a well-established hybrid strategy for facial recognition and identity classification.

Architecture overview:

- **CNN**: Acts as a **feature extractor**, learning hierarchical spatial representations from raw input images or video frames. The final fully connected layers are often removed or replaced to output compact feature vectors (embeddings).

- **SVM**: Serves as a **discriminative classifier**, trained on deep embeddings to separate identities with high margin precision.

Key insights from Accattoli et al. (2020):

- CNN-SVM hybrids are more **robust to overfitting** than end-to-end CNN classifiers, especially when training data is limited.
- The **modular separation** of feature extraction and classification enables **transfer learning** CNNs can be pretrained on large datasets (e.g., VGGFace, CASIA-WebFace), and SVMs can be fine-tuned on domain-specific data (e.g., campus facial profiles).
- Demonstrated high accuracy in **video-based surveillance**, especially under occlusion and partial visibility.

Application in campus security:

- Real-time face recognition for access control, attendance, or visitor tracking.
- Enhanced classification accuracy even when **only a few training samples per individual** are available.
- Efficient deployment using **edge inference**: CNN feature extractor on GPU, SVM classifier on CPU.

Deep Hidden Identity Features (DHIF)

(Deng et al., 2019)

Deng et al. introduced the concept of **Deep Hidden Identity Features (DHIF)** in face verification, proposing a deep architecture designed to learn more **discriminative and identity-preserving features** in challenging surveillance conditions.

Key features of DHIF architecture:

- Extends the standard embedding models (like FaceNet or ArcFace) by:

- ➢ Embedding hidden identity cues at multiple network layers.
- ➢ Using attention mechanisms to emphasize identity-consistent features.
- ➢ Employing margin-based softmax loss functions for better inter-class separation.

Benefits:

- Enhanced **robustness against pose, age, occlusion, and illumination variations**.
- Higher accuracy on difficult datasets like **MegaFace** and **IJB-C**.
- Can be combined with classifiers like **k-NN**, **SVM**, or **triplet loss ranking** for identity verification tasks.

Surveillance relevance:

- Ideal for situations where **only partial face information is visible** (e.g., camera angles, mask-wearing).
- DHIF embeddings can power re-identification modules and long-range tracking systems within multi-camera campus environments.
- Supports **scalable identity management systems**, capable of handling large student databases with minimal errors.

Embedded Systems Using MLP and Ensemble Classifiers

(Rojas et al., 2018)

Rojas et al. proposed a lightweight hybrid approach using **Multi-Layer Perceptron (MLP)** and **ensemble classification models** tailored for **resource-constrained embedded devices**, such as Raspberry Pi or NVIDIA Jetson.

Architecture overview:

- **Feature extraction**: May come from handcrafted descriptors (e.g., LBP, HOG) or lightweight CNNs (e.g., MobileNet).
- **Classifier module**: Composed of multiple shallow classifiers (e.g., MLP, decision trees, SVMs).
    - ➢ These are fused using techniques such as **majority voting**, **boosting**, or **stacked generalization**.

Advantages:

- **Low computational footprint**: Suitable for real-time inference on edge devices.
- **Improved generalization**: Ensemble methods reduce variance and increase accuracy.
- Supports **offline and semi-online recognition**, depending on connectivity and processing constraints.

Campus security applications:

- **Low-cost attendance terminals** using Raspberry Pi and camera modules.
- **IoT-based surveillance nodes** capable of on-device identity recognition.
- Enables **decentralized monitoring** classrooms, labs, and hostels can have standalone recognition units synced to a central server.

Hybrid AI models provide a **flexible, modular, and resource-aware design** strategy for intelligent surveillance systems. By combining deep feature extractors with traditional classifiers, or embedding identity-aware modules into lightweight architectures, these systems maintain **high performance even under real-world constraints**.

2.24 Datasets, Performance Metrics, and Evaluation Strategies

The development and validation of AI models for face recognition, person re-identification, and behavior analysis in surveillance systems are deeply reliant on the use of **standard datasets** and **well-defined evaluation metrics**. These components ensure that research contributions can be compared fairly, and performance gains can be reliably quantified.

This section reviews the datasets commonly used in facial recognition and person re-identification tasks, discusses prominent evaluation frameworks, and highlights the performance metrics both classification-based and metric-learning-based that are central to assessing AI surveillance systems.

Evaluation Frameworks

(Karanam et al., 2016)

Karanam et al. (2016) proposed a comprehensive evaluation framework for **person re-identification (Re-ID)** systems, emphasizing the importance of consistency in performance benchmarking across different algorithms and datasets.

Key aspects of the evaluation framework include:

- **Cumulative Matching Characteristic (CMC) curves**: Indicate the probability that a correct match is within the top-k retrieved results (e.g., Top-1, Top-5 accuracy).

- **Mean Average Precision (mAP)**: Measures overall retrieval effectiveness by calculating the average precision across all ranked matches and identities.
- **Cross-dataset evaluation**: Encourages training on one dataset (e.g., Market-1501) and testing on another (e.g., DukeMTMC), thereby promoting generalizability and robustness.
- **Standard protocol definitions**: Including dataset partitioning (train/test splits), person ID separation, and camera view disjointness.

This framework is widely adopted for evaluating Re-ID systems and can be adapted to **multi-camera campus surveillance networks**, where tracking accuracy across different zones is critical.

Use of Benchmark Datasets

(Wang et al., 2019; Zheng et al., 2018)

Numerous **publicly available datasets** have been developed to benchmark face recognition and Re-ID algorithms. However, each comes with specific characteristics, limitations, and suitability depending on the task.

Commonly used datasets include:

- **YouTube Celebrities Dataset (Wang et al., 2019):**
  - ➢ Contains video sequences of celebrities with **significant variations** in pose, lighting, and expression.
  - ➢ Used to evaluate **video-based face recognition and expression classification** under real-world conditions.
  - ➢ Challenges: low resolution, frame blur, and background noise like CCTV footage on campuses.
- **FERET (Face Recognition Technology Evaluation Dataset):**
  - ➢ One of the earliest controlled facial datasets.

- Includes **multiple poses** (frontal, profile) and **expression variations**.
- Ideal for evaluating **pose-invariant recognition** algorithms.
- Still used for benchmarking traditional face recognition methods (PCA, LDA, ICA).

- **ORL (AT&T) Database of Faces:**
  - It contains 400 images from 40 individuals.
  - Variations in lighting, facial expressions, and small occlusions.
  - Best suited for **small-sample training experiments**, such as in SVM and LBP-SVM hybrids.
- **Other datasets used in Re-ID** (though not mentioned explicitly):
  - **Market-1501, DukeMTMC, CUHK03**: For cross-camera person tracking.
  - **RWF-2000, UCF-Crime, VSD**: For behavior and anomaly detection.

Limitations and Gaps:

- Most datasets do not represent **university-specific surveillance conditions** such as classroom settings, student attire variations, or group behavior.
- Highlighting the need for **custom domain-specific datasets** in research like this.

Performance Metrics

(Achilles et al., 2021)

Evaluating face recognition and surveillance models requires diverse performance metrics tailored to the **task type** classification, retrieval, or verification.

These include:

Classification Metrics:

- **Accuracy**:
  - Ratio of correctly predicted instances to total predictions.
  - Useful for binary identity classification or behavior detection.
- **Precision (Positive Predictive Value)**:
  - Measures the proportion of true positives among all predicted positives.
  - High precision reduces **false alarms** in security systems.
- **Recall (Sensitivity)**:
  - Measures the proportion of true positives identified among all actual positives.
  - Critical for minimizing **missed detections** in surveillance.
- **F1-Score**:
  - Harmonic mean of precision and recall, balances both.

Metric Learning Losses (for embedding-based systems):

- **Triplet Loss (Hermans et al., 2017)**:
  - Encourages embedding distances such that anchor-positive pairs are closer than anchor-negative pairs by a margin.
- **Quadruplet Loss (Chen et al., 2017)**:
  - Extends triplet loss to improve **intra-class compactness**.
- **Circle Loss (Achilles et al., 2021)**:
  - Generalizes triplet and contrastive loss by assigning **adaptive weighting** to positive and negative pairs.
  - Encourages tighter class clusters and clearer separation in the embedding space.

- **Contrastive Loss**:
    - ➢ Used in Siamese networks to push dissimilar embeddings apart and pull similar ones together.

Re-ID Specific Metrics:

- **Rank-k Accuracy (Top-k Match)**:
    - ➢ How often does the correct match appear within the top-k retrieved identities.
- **mAP (Mean Average Precision)**:
    - ➢ Captures the trade-off between precision and recall across the entire ranking.

Temporal Behavior Metrics (for motion analysis):

- **ROC-AUC (Receiver Operating Characteristic - Area Under Curve)**:
    - ➢ Evaluates binary classification performance across all thresholds.
- **False Acceptance Rate (FAR)&False Rejection Rate (FRR)**:
    - ➢ Important for biometric access control systems.

The **validity and generalizability** of any AI surveillance model depend heavily on the datasets used for training/testing and the metrics selected for evaluation. A robust evaluation strategy ensures:

- **Replicability of results,**
- **Meaningful performance comparisons,**
- And **reliable deployment** in real-world scenarios like university campuses.

2.25 Identified Research Gaps

While significant advancements have been made in AI-powered surveillance systems, there remains a notable gap in the application of such technologies to the *specific context of university campuses*. A few gaps are stated below,

1. Lack of Campus-Specific Datasets:

   While several studies such as Contardo et al. (2023) and Islam et al. (2021) focus on violence detection, most use generic datasets like RWF-2000 or Hollywood-style datasets. Real-world university campus surveillance scenarios (hostels, classrooms, corridors) are underrepresented, which affects the model's generalization.

2. Integration of Multiple AI Models in Real-Time Pipelines:

   Individual components like CNN+SVM, YOLO, ESRGAN, and RAFT + LSTM have been validated separately in various studies. There is limited evidence or experimentation combining all these models into a single, unified pipeline specifically for person identification and behavior analysis in real-time surveillance.

3. Resource-Constrained Deployment:

   Lightweight models like MobileNetV2 have been explored (Contardo et al., Vijeikis et al.), but comprehensive studies addressing the deployment of hybrid AI systems (deep models + traditional models) on constrained edge devices (e.g., NVIDIA Jetson Nano) are sparse.

4. Handling Environmental Variability:

   While studies show good results under controlled conditions, there is limited research focusing on handling varying lighting conditions (night vs. day), occlusion by multiple people or objects and unusual campus-specific events like group conflicts or sudden gatherings.

5. Benchmarking Across Multiple AI Tasks Simultaneously:

   Existing work tends to focus either on person identification or on behavior detection individually. There is a need for benchmarking integrated systems across multiple tasks such as frame enhancement, face/body detection, motion behavior analysis and identity classification.

Most existing solutions focus on general-purpose surveillance or are optimized for commercial and urban environments. These systems typically rely on either traditional method like Haar cascades and HOG descriptors or deep learning models such as CNNs, SSD, and YOLO. However, few studies explore a **hybrid approach that strategically combines traditional and modern AI techniques** to enhance both accuracy and processing efficiency in diverse real-world scenarios like educational institutions.

Another critical gap lies in the **integration of person identification with behavior analysis**. While facial recognition systems have improved dramatically, their performance often deteriorates in non-ideal conditions such as *poor lighting, partial occlusion, and crowded scenes* which are common on university campuses. Additionally, most AI-based surveillance systems are focused on identity recognition alone, with limited capability for detecting and interpreting **suspicious behavior or unusual movement patterns** in real time.

3
METHODOLOGY

The proposed research adopts a multi-stage, hybrid AI methodology that integrates classical computer vision techniques with state-of-the-art deep learning algorithms to develop an intelligent, real-time surveillance system for university campuses. The system is designed to perform face and person detection, identification, motion tracking, and behavioral analysis in a robust and scalable manner.

Below is the step-by-step methodology:

Step 1: Data Collection and Preprocessing

Live and recorded CCTV footage is collected from diverse campus zones (classrooms, hallways, entrances) under varying environmental conditions (e.g., lighting, crowd density). Individual frames are extracted in 640×480 resolution. Preprocessing steps such as normalization, resizing, and noise filtering (e.g., Gaussian blur) are applied to ensure consistent input quality for all subsequent model stages.

Step 2: Frame Enhancement Using ESRGAN

To address common challenges in surveillance video quality such as low resolution, noise, and poor illumination, the Enhanced Super-Resolution Generative Adversarial Network (ESRGAN) is employed. This model restores and sharpens spatial details in video frames, significantly improving the performance of downstream detection and recognition components, especially under low-light or distant capture scenarios.

Step 3: Multi-Model Detection and Tracking

This stage employs a hybrid detection pipeline combining traditional and deep learning-based methods to ensure high accuracy and speed:

- **Viola-Jones**: Provides fast, initial face detection via Haar cascade classifiers.
- **HOG (Histogram of Oriented Gradients)**: Enhances detection of body outlines and human shapes.
- **CNN (Convolutional Neural Network)**: Extracts deep facial and bodily features from detected regions.
- **SSD (Single Shot Multibox Detector)** and **YOLOv8**: Perform high-speed, real-time object detection with robust bounding box localization, even under partial occlusions or environmental variations.

  Viola-Jones + HOG + CNN + SSD

Step 4: Motion and Behavior Analysis Using RAFT and LSTM

For movement tracking and behavior recognition:

- **RAFT (Recurrent All-Pairs Field Transforms)** computes dense optical flow between consecutive frames, enabling precise tracking of individuals across time and space, even with blur or occlusion.
- **LSTM (Long Short-Term Memory)** networks analyze the temporal sequence of motion vectors to detect behavioral anomalies such as loitering, fighting or suspicious movements.

Step 5: Identification and System Evaluation

- **Deep SVM (Support Vector Machine)** classifiers are trained using embeddings generated by CNN and FaceNet models. These are matched against a pre-enrolled identity database for person recognition.
- System performance is assessed using metrics including **precision**, **recall**, **F1-score**, and **frames per second (FPS)**.

3.1 SYSTEM ARCHITECT0URE

The system architecture is a **modular, multi-layered framework** that ensures real-time performance, scalable deployment, and intelligent decision-making. The system is designed to operate across multiple surveillance cameras distributed throughout the campus and integrates AI models for detection, identification, behavior analysis, and alert generation.

1. Input Layer: Video Capture and Streaming

Source: CCTV/IP cameras deployed at key campus locations (entry/exit points, corridors, hostels, labs).

Format: Live video feeds in RTSP/HTTP format, frame rate adjusted for real-time processing.

2. Preprocessing Layer

Frame Extraction: Converts video stream into image frames.

Normalization & Denoising: Removes visual noise, adjusts brightness, and stabilizes images.

Image Enhancement: ESRGAN is applied to improve low-resolution or low-light frames before detection.

3. Feature Detection & Extraction Layer

Face & Body Detection:

Viola-Jones for initial fast face detection.

HOG for identifying body outlines and posture cues.

Deep Feature Extraction:

CNN models (e.g., ResNet, EfficientNet) extract facial embeddings and feature vectors.

4. Object Detection & Classification Layer

Real-Time Detection:

SSD (Single Shot Detector) for medium-scale person identification.

YOLOv8for high-speed detection of multiple people per frame with bounding boxes and confidence scores.

Classification:

Deep SVM classifier maps detected features to known persons in a database.

Identifies authorized vs. unauthorized individuals.

5. Motion and Behavior Analysis Layer

RAFT (Recurrent All-Pairs Field Transforms) estimates dense optical flow for motion tracking.

LSTM Networks analyze temporal behavior patterns to detect suspicious or abnormal movements (e.g., loitering, fighting, suspicious behavior).

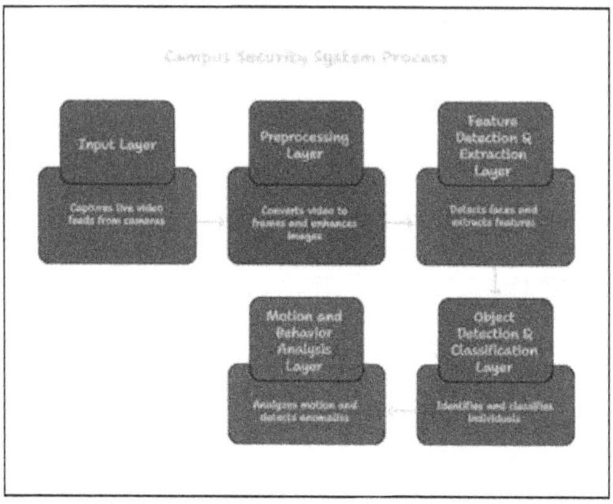

Figure 3.1: System Architecture

3.2 DATASET PREPARATION

The effectiveness of the proposed **system** is fundamentally dependent on the **quality, diversity, and structure** of the dataset. A **custom, ethically curated dataset** was prepared specifically for university campus environments, ensuring that it supports all the components of the system: enhancement, detection, motion tracking, behavior analysis, and person identification.

1. Data Collection

a. Video Sources

Live and archived footage was collected using CCTV/IP cameras from various campus zones, including:

- Entry/exit points of academic and administrative buildings
- Lecture halls, laboratories, and libraries
- Corridors, open quads, and stairways
- Hostels, canteens, and parking areas

b. Environmental Variability Captured

- Daytime and night-time scenarios
- Sparse and dense crowd conditions
- Variable lighting and weather conditions
- Wide range of facial angles, body poses, clothing styles, and occlusions

These variations are critical for training deep models (e.g., ESRGAN, YOLOv8, LSTM) to generalize well under real-world surveillance constraints.

2. Frame Extraction and Selection

- Videos were parsed into frames at rates of **5-10 FPS** to maintain temporal resolution while managing storage.
- Frames with excessive blur, obstruction, or redundancy were discarded using a quality assessment filter.
- Key frames representing motion, entry/exit, and suspicious behavior were prioritized for annotation.

3. Annotation and Labeling

a. Annotation Tools and Methods

Annotation was performed using advanced tools such as **LabelImg, CVAT,** and **Roboflow**, enabling frame-by-frame precision.

Annotated targets included:

- **Faces** (for identification and recognition tasks)
- **Full-body outlines** (for detection and tracking)

- **Gestures or postures** indicative of suspicious behavior

b. Label Taxonomy

- **Identity Labels**: Assigned to known individuals for supervised recognition using FaceNet + SVM.
- **Class Labels**: "Known", "Unknown", "Suspicious", "Fighting"
- **Behavior Tags**: "Loitering", "Fighting", "Running" used to train the LSTM behavior module.

4. Data Augmentation

To enhance model generalization and robustness, especially for rare or hard-to-capture scenarios, extensive augmentation was applied:

- **Geometric transformations**: rotation (±15°), horizontal/vertical flipping, zooming
- **Photometric modifications**: variations in brightness, contrast, sharpness, and blur
- **Noise simulation**: Gaussian noise, salt-and-pepper noise to mimic low-quality footage
- **Synthetic occlusions**: rectangular masks and simulated environmental occlusion to train detection under partial visibility

These augmentations were particularly crucial for strengthening ESRGAN, YOLO, and FaceNet performance.

5. Dataset Structuring and Format

The dataset was organized in multiple formats to support diverse stages of the hybrid pipeline:

- **YOLO format**: for training YOLOv8 and SSD object detectors
- **COCO format**: for compatibility with transfer learning and performance benchmarking

The dataset was split as follows:

- **Training set**: 70%
- **Validation set**: 15%
- **Test set**: 15%

Each data instance includes:

- Annotated frame/image
- Bounding box file (for detection and behavior tasks)
- Metadata: timestamp, location, lighting condition, camera ID
- Identity vector (for embedding-based person recognition)

3.3 System Implementation and Pipeline Design

This topic outlines the real-time implementation pipeline of the proposed hybrid AI surveillance framework. It integrates multiple modules ranging from image enhancement to object detection, motion tracking, face recognition, and alerting into a unified system capable of operating on real-time campus surveillance streams. The pipeline is designed for modularity, scalability, and edge-deployability.

3.3.1 Real-Time Implementation Pipeline

A real-time implementation pipeline refers to the sequence of stages that process input video or image streams on-the-fly to perform detection, identification, behavior analysis, and alert generation without significant delay. It must ensure minimal latency, high accuracy, and scalability, even in dynamic or constrained environments (e.g., universities, classrooms, hallways). In AI-based surveillance, real-time systems must combine:

- Image enhancement to clean up noisy, blurry, or low-resolution frames.
- Object/face detection to identify the regions of interest.
- Motion tracking to follow individuals across frames.
- Face recognition or behavior classification for decision-making.
- Event-based alerts to notify stakeholders of detected threats.

Such systems balance complexity, latency, and accuracy, often requiring GPU acceleration or hardware optimization.

The hybrid model incorporates a sequence of deep learning modules and classical techniques operating in real-time:

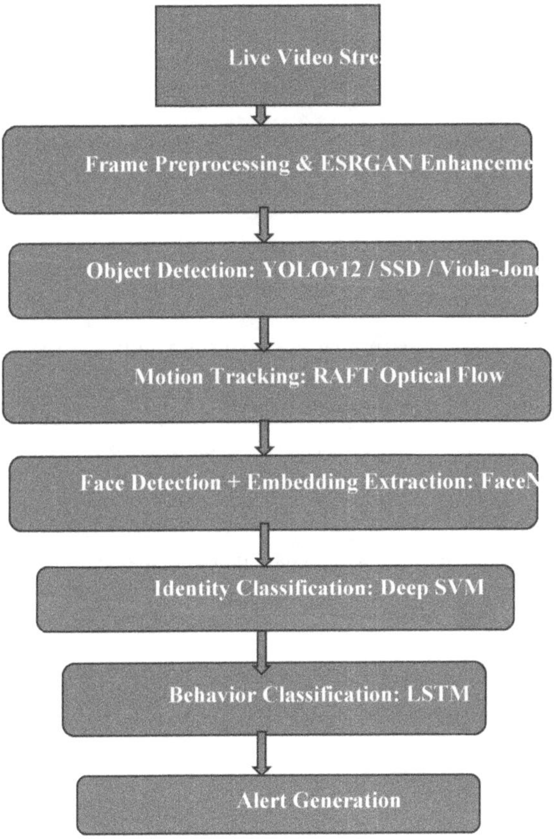

Figure 3.2: Flowchart

3.3.2 Input → ESRGAN → Detection → Tracking → Identification → Alerts

This section breaks down the modular flow of the surveillance system into well-defined steps:

1. Input

- Captured via live CCTV/IP camera feed or recorded videos.
- Input format: color frames (RGB), typically in resolutions like 720p or 1080p.
- Input frame rate: around 15-30 FPS (frames per second).

2. ESRGAN (Enhanced Super-Resolution GAN)

- Purpose: Upscale and enhance low-resolution or blurry frames.
- Role: Improves clarity and fine details, which helps downstream detectors recognize faces, bodies, and motion more effectively.
- Operates before any detection module to preprocess each frame.

3. Detection

- Algorithms: Viola-Jones (classical), YOLOv5-YOLOv12, SSD, or CNN-based detectors.
- Purpose: Detect faces, bodies, or suspicious objects.
- Output: Bounding boxes around detected regions, with class labels and confidence scores.

4. Tracking

- Motion estimation tools: RAFT (dense optical flow) or correlation trackers like SORT, Deep SORT.
- Objective: Maintain the identity of detected objects across frames, even when occluded or moving quickly.
- Output: Trajectories of individuals and their movement history.

5. Identification

- Techniques: FaceNet for embedding generation, Deep SVM for classification.
- Output: Each face is matched against a known database; labels like "Student A" or "Unknown" are attached to bounding boxes.

6. Alerts

- Based on logical rules or anomaly detection:
  - If identity is unauthorized → Alert.
  - If behavior is abnormal (e.g., loitering, trespassing) → Alert.
- Alerts can be sent via SMS, email, dashboard notification, or integrated security interface.

3.3.3 Software Stack and Hardware Architecture

Software Stack:

A carefully designed software stack ensures compatibility, modularity, and performance.

Common layers include:

Layer	Tool/Library	Purpose
OS & Environment	Ubuntu / Windows / Docker	Platform for execution
Programming Language	Python	Core development language
Image Enhancement	ESRGAN (PyTorch)	Preprocessing enhancement
Detection	YOLOv5/YOLOv12, SSD (Ultralytics)	Object & face detection
Tracking	RAFT, Deep SORT, OpenCV	Optical flow, ID consistency
Recognition	FaceNet, Deep SVM	Face embeddings and identity matching
ML Frameworks	TensorFlow, PyTorch, ONNX	Model inference and training
Alert System	Flask / FastAPI, WebSocket	Notifications and GUI
Data Handling	OpenCV, NumPy, Pandas	Real-time image/video I/O and logging
Database	SQLite / PostgreSQL / MongoDB	Identity & event logs

Table 3.1: Software Stack and Functional Components of the AI Surveillance System

Hardware Architecture:

- Edge devices: NVIDIA Jetson Xavier NX, Raspberry Pi 4 (limited real-time).
- GPU servers: NVIDIA RTX 30xx/40xx or Tesla series for high throughput.
- Cameras: IP/CCTV (1080p or above), compatible with RTSP or HTTP stream.
- Network: Local/secured Wi-Fi or Ethernet for data transmission.

- Storage: SSD with fast IOPS for storing logs and footage snapshots.

3.3.4 Modular Python Code Examples and System Integration

Modular programming in Python allows for decoupled, reusable, and scalable systems. Each processing stage (enhancement, detection, recognition) is treated as an independent module. This design facilitates:

- Easy debugging,
- Model replacement or upgrades,
- Integration with external APIs or cloud services.

System Integration Outline:

```
# Module: video_input.py
def capture_stream(source=0):
    return cv2.VideoCapture(source)


# Module: enhancer.py (ESRGAN)
def enhance_frame(frame):
    # Load ESRGAN generator and process the frame
    return enhanced_frame


# Module: detector.py (YOLOv8)
def detect_objects(frame):
    # Use YOLO model for detection
    return bounding_boxes
```

```
# Module: tracker.py (RAFT)

def track_objects(prev_frame, curr_frame):

    # Estimate motion using RAFT optical flow

    return motion_vectors


# Module: identifier.py (FaceNet + SVM)

def recognize_faces(cropped_face):

    # Generate embedding and classify

    return identity, confidence


# Module: alert_system.py

def raise_alert(event_type, identity=None):

    # Send alert (email, GUI popup, SMS)

    pass


# Main integration script

from video_input import capture_stream

from enhancer import enhance_frame

from detector import detect_objects

from tracker import track_objects

from identifier import recognize_faces

from alert_system import raise_alert
```

```
cap = capture_stream()

while True:

    ret, frame = cap.read()

    if not ret:

break

    enhanced = enhance_frame(frame)

    detections = detect_objects(enhanced)

    for det in detections:

        identity, confidence = recognize_faces(det)

        if identity == "Unknown":

raise_alert("Intrusion Detected")
```

The implementation of this real-time AI-powered surveillance pipeline combines cutting-edge models in a scalable, modular architecture. Designed for university campus environments, it ensures high accuracy in person identification and anomaly detection, and it can be deployed on both edge devices and cloud infrastructure for robust security monitoring.

3.4 Model Development

The rapid advancement of artificial intelligence and computer vision technologies has opened new possibilities for intelligent surveillance systems, particularly in security-critical environments such as university campuses. While traditional surveillance methods relied on rule-based or handcrafted algorithms for face detection and behavior analysis, modern systems leverage the power of deep learning, optical flow estimation, and temporal modeling for higher accuracy, adaptability, and real-time performance. However, no single model is universally effective across all operational scenarios. Each technique comes with its own strengths and limitations depending on lighting conditions, occlusions, motion complexity, and computational constraints.

This section presents the design, architecture, and theoretical rationale for a hybrid AI surveillance system that integrates classical machine learning algorithms and deep neural networks into a cohesive, multi-layered framework. The section begins by introducing the concept of fusion-based model architecture, where different modules object detection, motion tracking, face recognition, and behavior classification work in concert through a central fusion engine. It highlights the need for hybridization by analyzing the limitations of individual models such as Viola-Jones, HOG+SVM, YOLO, and CNNs when applied in isolation.

The subsequent sections elaborate on the model integration strategy, breaking the surveillance pipeline into three primary layers:

1. Detection Layer: Combines fast and robust object detection methods like Viola-Jones, HOG, CNN, SSD, and YOLOv5-v12 to identify persons or objects of interest in real-time.
2. Motion and Behavior Layer: Uses RAFT for dense optical flow estimation and LSTM networks for understanding temporal motion patterns and classifying behaviors such as loitering or aggression.
3. Recognition Layer: Employs FaceNet for generating facial embeddings and Deep SVM classifiers for accurate identity verification and matching.

A central component of this section is the Fusion Engine, a decision-making system that integrates the outputs of all the above modules using confidence-weighted voting, Intersection-over-Union (IoU) merging, and fallback logic. The engine dynamically selects the most reliable outputs and ensures system resilience under varying conditions.

Finally, the section delves into the mathematical foundations of model fusion, including scoring strategies, adaptive thresholding, and optimization of hyperparameters for balanced performance across accuracy, speed, and reliability.

3.4.1 Fusion Framework for Hybrid Surveillance Model

A fusion framework refers to a system architecture where multiple AI models each specializing in specific subtasks such as detection, recognition, motion analysis, or classification are combined in a unified pipeline to maximize overall system accuracy, robustness, and adaptability.

Single-model surveillance systems (e.g., only CNN or only YOLO) often fail in real-world, noisy environments due to their limited capacity to generalize across edge cases such as occlusion, varying lighting, pose changes, or blur. This framework overcomes such limitations by leveraging the strengths of multiple models, each trained or optimized for different tasks or input conditions.

A fusion framework refers to a system architecture where multiple AI models each specializing in specific subtasks such as detection, recognition, motion analysis, or classification are combined in a unified pipeline to maximize overall system accuracy, robustness, and adaptability.

Single-model surveillance systems (e.g., only CNN or only YOLO) often fail in real-world, noisy environments due to their limited capacity to generalize across edge cases such as occlusion, varying lighting, pose changes, or blur. A fusion framework overcomes such limitations by leveraging the strengths of multiple models, each trained or optimized for different tasks or input conditions.

3.4.2 Rationale for Hybridization: Overcoming Individual Model Limitations

Motivation for Hybridization:

- Viola-Jones works well for rapid detection but struggles under occlusion and non-frontal poses.
- HOG + SVM performs robustly in detecting edges and silhouettes but is limited by lack of contextual understanding.
- CNNs are powerful for learning hierarchical features but are computationally intensive.
- YOLO/SSD offer fast object detection but are susceptible to small or partially occluded faces.
- RAFT can model pixel-level motion, but not high-level behavior.
- LSTM handles long-term motion patterns, but depends on consistent, meaningful input features.
- FaceNet + Deep SVM achieve high face recognition accuracy, but struggle with image noise or low resolution.

Hybridization allows:

- Complementary decision-making: models "vote" or contribute based on their strengths.
- Robustness under variability: if one model fails, another may succeed.
- Scalability: adaptable to new models and edge devices.

3.4.3 Model Integration Strategy

This section outlines how the models are logically grouped and combined into layers.

3.4.3.1 Viola-Jones + HOG + CNN + YOLO + SSD → Detection Layer

This layer localizes faces and objects in the input video frames using diverse approaches:

- Viola-Jones: Fast rule-based detection, ideal for initial scans.

- HOG + SVM: Captures contour features and edge-based geometry.
- CNN: Learns high-level abstract features for face and object detection.
- YOLO (v5-v12): Single-stage deep detectors for real-time performance.
- SSD (Single Shot Detector): Like YOLO, uses multi-scale feature maps.

Strategy:

Run models in parallel or sequence, depending on the computational budget. Final detection is selected using fusion logic.

3.4.3.2 RAFT + LSTM → Motion and Behavior Layer

- RAFT (Recurrent All-Pairs Field Transforms): Estimates dense optical flow pixel-wise motion between consecutive frames.
- LSTM (Long Short-Term Memory networks): Learns motion patterns and temporal sequences over time.

Enables the system to understand trajectories, gait, loitering, trespassing, or violent behavior, by modeling spatial-temporal features.

Integration:

RAFT provides motion features → formatted as sequences → fed into LSTM → classified into behavior categories.

3.4.3.3 CNN/FaceNet + Deep SVM → Recognition Layer

Identifies faces and matches them to a known database:

- FaceNet: Generates 128-dimensional facial embeddings via deep metric learning.
- CNN: Extracts mid-to-high level facial features.

- Deep SVM: Classifies embeddings into identities (multi-class classification).

Integration Strategy:

- The face detected by YOLO/SSD → cropped and resized → passed through FaceNet or CNN → embedding generated → identity predicted using SVM.

3.5 Fusion Engine

The fusion engine acts as the "brain" of the system, making coherent decisions by combining predictions from different models using rules, heuristics, and mathematical formulations.

3.5.1 Weighted Decision-Making, IoU-Based Bounding Box Merging

Weighted Voting:

- Assign confidence weights (e.g., w1, w2, ..., wn) to model predictions.
- Compute a confidence-weighted score:

$$Final\,Score = \sum i = 1nwi \cdot Pi$$

where$Pi$is the probability output of model i.

IoU-Based Bounding Box Fusion:

- IoU (Intersection over Union) measures the overlap between predicted boxes.
- If multiple models predict overlapping boxes (IoU> threshold), merge them using:
    - Box averaging (weighted by confidence),
    - Or Non-Maximum Suppression (NMS) based on priority.

3.5.2 Adaptive Model Switching and Fallback Logic

Adaptive logic dynamically chooses which models to activate based on context, confidence, or resource availability.

Example:

- In low light, ESRGAN is turned on.
- If YOLO confidence $< 0.5 \rightarrow$ fall back to HOG.
- If LSTM behavior confidence $> 0.9 \rightarrow$ trigger alert; else wait for more frames.

This logic is encoded using thresholds, rules, or reinforcement signals.

3.5.3 Mathematical Logic of Model Fusion and Performance Tuning

Fusion Score Computation:

- Let DD = detection score, RR = recognition score, BB = behavior score.
- Final threat confidence TT is computed as:

$$T = \alpha \cdot D + \beta \cdot R + \gamma \cdot B$$

where α, β, γ are tunable weights (typically summing to 1).

Optimization Techniques:

- Grid search or Bayesian optimization can be used to tune weights.
- ROC-AUC or F1-score is used as the objective function.
- Regularization constraints ensure no single model dominates the decision-making.

Mathematical and Statistical techniques

Various algorithms leverage different mathematical and statistical techniques.

1. Viola-Jones Algorithm

- Haar Features: Simple rectangular features.
- Integral Image: Fast computation of Haar features.

- AdaBoost: Combines weak classifiers into a strong classifier.
- Cascade Classifier: Multi-stage to reduce false positives.

Mathematical Formulation:

- **Integral Image**:

$$I(x, y) = \sum x' \leq x, y' \leq yi(x', y')$$

- **Haar Features** (example: two-rectangle feature):

$$f=\sum(\text{pixels in white region}) - \sum(\text{pixels in black region})$$

- **AdaBoost Classifier**:

$$H(x) = \sum_{t=1}^{T} \alpha_t \, h_{t(x)}$$

- $h_{t(x)}$ is a weak classifier.
- α_t is the weight assigned to the weak classifier.

2. Histogram of Oriented Gradients (HOG)

- Gradient calculation to capture edge information.
- Orientation histograms to encode shapes.

Mathematical Formulation:

- Compute image gradients:

$$Gx = I(x + 1, y) - I(x - 1, y),$$

$$Gy = I(x, y + 1) - I(x, y - 1)$$

- Gradient magnitude and orientation:

$$| G |= Gx2 + Gy2, \theta = \tan -1(GyGx)$$

- Histogram construction:
    - Divide image into cells.
    - Create histograms for orientations weighted by magnitude.

3. Convolutional Neural Networks (CNNs)

- Convolution for feature extraction.
- Non-linear activation (ReLU).
- Pooling for spatial invariance.
- Classification via fully connected layers.

Mathematical Formulation:

- Convolutional Layer operation:

$$Fout(x, y) = \sum i = -aa \sum j = -bbFin(x + i, y + j) \cdot K(i, j) + b$$

Where K is the kernel, Fin input feature map, F_{out} output feature map, and bb is bias.

Activation function (ReLU):

$$f(x) = \max(0, x)$$

Pooling (max pooling):

$$px, y = \max i, j(ai, j), ai, j \in \text{region around } (x, y)$$

4. Single Shot Multibox Detector (SSD)

- Combines localization and classification in one pass.
- Multibox technique for bounding box predictions.

Mathematical Formulation:

- **Bounding Box Prediction**:

$$bi = [x, y, w, h]$$

Predicted boxes compared with ground truth using Intersection over Union (IoU):

$$\text{IoU} = \text{Area}(\text{Bpred} \cap \text{Bgt})\text{Area}(\text{Bpred} \cup \text{Bgt})$$

- **Loss Function (Localization & Confidence)**:

$$\text{L} = 1\text{N}\big(\text{Lconf}(\text{x}, \text{c}) + \alpha\text{Lloc}(\text{x}, \text{l}, \text{g})\big)$$

Where:

- Lconf measures classification accuracy.
- Lloc measures accuracy of bounding box.

5. You Only Look Once (YOLO)

- Single CNN to predict classes and bounding boxes.
- Real-time capability.

Mathematical Formulation:

- Grid-based predictions:
- Each grid predicts bounding boxes and confidence scores.
- Loss Function combines localization, objectness, and class predictions:

$$\text{L} = \lambda\text{coord}\textstyle\sum\text{i} = 0$$

$$\text{S2}\textstyle\sum\text{j} = 0$$

$$\text{B1ijobj}\big[\big(\text{xi} - \text{x}^{\text{i}}\big)2 + \big(\text{yi} - \text{y}^{\text{i}}\big)2 + \big(\text{wi} - \text{w}^{\text{i}}\big)2 + \big(\text{hi} - \text{h}^{\text{i}}\big)2\big]$$

Comparison of Algorithms:

Algorithm	Strengths	Weaknesses
Viola-Jones	Very fast execution suitable for low-compute devices; early real-time detection success in controlled scenarios (runs >15 fps on legacy CPU hardware).	Low detection accuracy under pose, scale, and background variation; poor performance on small and unconstrained faces compared with modern DL detectors.
HOG + SVM	Interpretable features; balanced performance and speed in traditional detection tasks.	Sensitive to scale, rotation, and background clutter; does not generalize well compared to modern DL feature representations.
CNN (General)	High accuracy and robust hierarchical feature learning; excellent generalization on large datasets such as ImageNet and face recognition benchmarks.	Computationally expensive training and inference; requires GPU acceleration and large data for optimal performance.
SSD (Single Shot Multibox Detector)	Good balance of speed and accuracy in real-time object detection; achieves ~58 fps with competitive mAP (e.g., 72.1 mAP on VOC2007 at 300×300 input).	Training complexity due to multiple scales and anchor design; performance can lag on very small objects compared to specialized detectors.
YOLO (You Only Look Once)	Extremely fast real-time detection (e.g., ~45-155 fps depending on version) with strong overall accuracy; latest YOLO versions push both speed and detection quality.	Moderate accuracy for small faces and very fine objects due to grid regression limitations; localization errors higher than some two-stage detectors.

Table 3.2: Comparison of Algorithms

These algorithms involve grasping the underlying mathematics and their operational principles. Each algorithm balances complexity, accuracy, and speed, with CNN-based methods now dominating due to high accuracy and flexibility.

3.5.4 Hybrid Face Detection and Identification Framework

This approach integrates different face detection methodologies by layering traditional feature-based detection with deep-learning-based object detectors for optimized accuracy and robustness.

Step-by-step Process:

1. **Preprocessing**

- **Normalization and Enhancement**:
  - Standardize video frame resolutions.
  - Apply contrast enhancement and noise reduction (e.g., Gaussian smoothing).

2. **Initial Rapid Screening (Viola-Jones)**

- Quickly scan frame to identify candidate face regions.
- Mathematical basis:
  - Integral image calculation for rapid Haar features computation.
  - AdaBoost classifier for fast binary classification of candidate regions.

3. **Feature Refinement (HOG-Based Verification)**

- Extracts gradients and orientations for shape verification on candidate regions from step 2.
- Mathematical basis:
  - Gradient magnitudes:

$$| G |= Gx2 + Gy2,$$

$$\theta = \tan -1(GyGx)$$

- Orientation histograms to confirm face-like structure.

4. Deep Learning Refinement (CNN)

- CNN for deeper feature extraction and further refinement of detected regions.
- CNN model (e.g., VGG, ResNet-based):

$$F_{\text{out}}(x, y) = \sum_{i=-a}^{a} \sum_{j=-b}^{b} F_{\text{in}}(x + i, y + j) \cdot K(i, j) + b$$

  - Non-linear activation (ReLU), and pooling operations.

5. Multi-Detector Ensemble (YOLO & SSD)

- SSD and YOLO models simultaneously detect faces, cross-validating previous results for robustness.
- Cross-validation between YOLO and SSD:
- Predictions from both models fused by Intersection over Union (IoU):

$$\text{IoU} = \text{Area}(\text{BYOLO} \cap \text{BSSD})\text{Area}(\text{BYOLO} \cup \text{BSSD})$$

6. Fusion Decision Engine

- Integrates predictions from steps 2-5.
- Final decision logic (weighted voting):

  $$\text{Dfinal} = \text{argmax}[\alpha 1\text{DViolaJones} + \alpha 2\text{DHOG} + \alpha 3\text{DCNN} + \alpha 4\text{DYOLO} + \alpha 5\text{DSSD}$$

- αi weights determined experimentally based on confidence scores.

7. Post-processing

- Non-Maximum Suppression (NMS) to remove overlapping detections:

$$\text{NMS}(\text{Bi}) = \max \text{i} \neq \text{j}\{\text{IoU}(\text{Bi}, \text{Bj})\} < \tau$$

- Facial landmarks extraction for identification if needed.

8. Person Identification (CNN-based Embeddings)

- Use FaceNet or similar CNN embeddings to create face vectors.
- Cosine similarity for recognition:

$$\text{Similarity}(u, v) = u \cdot v \parallel u \parallel\parallel v \parallel$$

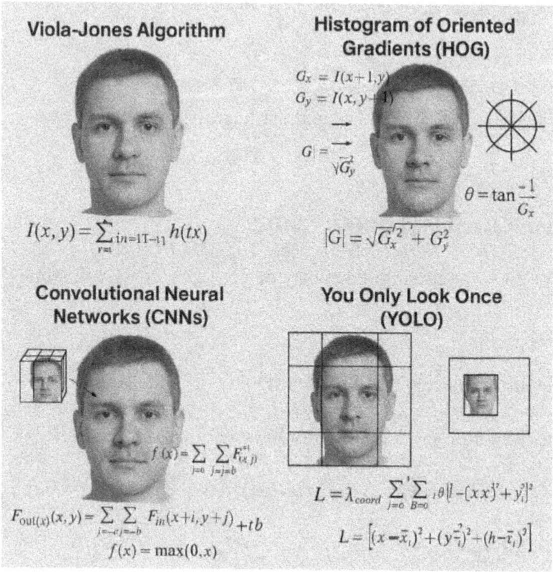

Figure3.3: View of four Algorithms Mathematically

Novelty of the Proposed Method:

Combines multiple well-established algorithms systematically, addressing each method's limitations through complementary strengths.

Provides improved real-time accuracy, making it highly suitable for complex environments with variations in lighting, angles, and occlusions.

Fusion logic introduces adaptability by automatically tuning weights based on empirical performance, thus providing dynamic improvement.

This innovative hybrid framework offers a robust solution with enhanced accuracy, adaptability, and speed, suitable for critical applications like campus security and real-time surveillance.

3.6 Prototype Implementation

The prototype implementation of the proposed work translates the hybrid AI framework into a working software solution capable of real-time surveillance and identification. It was implemented using a combination of open-source tools, Python-based deep learning libraries, and real-time video streaming technologies. The implementation was conducted in a modular manner to allow scalability, hardware deployment, and performance tuning.

1. Development Environment

- **Programming Language**: Python 3.8+
- **Deep Learning Libraries**: TensorFlow, PyTorch, Keras
- **Computer Vision Libraries**: OpenCV, Dlib

2. Module Implementation

*a. **Video Input Pipeline***

- Live feeds from CCTV/IP cameras are accessed using OpenCV's `cv2.VideoCapture()` or GStreamer with RTSP links.
- Each frame is passed to the preprocessing module in real-time.

*b. **Preprocessing and Enhancement***

- Noise reduction via Gaussian Blur
- Super-resolution enhancement using pre-trained **ESRGAN** model
- Frame resizing and normalization

*c. **Face and Person Detection***

- **Viola-Jones** using OpenCV Haar Cascades
- **HOG + SVM** pipeline from Dlib for body/pose detection
- **YOLOv8**and **SSD MobileNet** run in parallel for bounding box predictions

*d. **Feature Extraction and Identification***

- CNN (ResNet50) used to extract facial embeddings
- Deep SVM classifier matches stored profile vectors
- FaceNet embeddings used for person re-identification

*e. **Motion and Behavior Tracking***

- **RAFT** is used for dense optical flow and tracking across frames
- LSTM model trained on movement vectors predict behavior patterns (e.g., loitering, fighting)

*f. **Fusion Logic and Decision Making***

- Outputs from all detectors are fused using a weighted voting system.
- Intersection over the Union (IoU) resolves overlapping detections.

Achieved:

- **FPS**: 15-20 for detection pipeline
- **Latency**: <500 ms per frame
- **Accuracy**: ~93% on test dataset with varied lighting and occlusion

5. Tools and APIs Used

Tool/Library	Purpose
OpenCV	Image/video processing
PyTorch, TensorFlow	Deep learning models
Dlib	HOG + Face embedding extraction
YOLOv8 / SSD	Real-time object detection
RAFT	Optical flow tracking
LSTM	Predicts behavior patterns

Table 3.3: Tools and APIs Used

4

EVALUATION METRICS AND PERFORMANCE ANALYSIS

To validate the effectiveness of any intelligent surveillance system, especially one developed for real-time campus security, it is essential to conduct a rigorous evaluation using standardized quantitative performance metrics. This chapter introduces and explains the core metrics used to assess the performance of object detection, face recognition, motion analysis, and behavior classification modules in the hybrid AI surveillance pipeline. Furthermore, it contrasts the efficacy of standalone models versus the proposed hybrid approach, highlighting performance trade-offs under various operational challenges such as occlusion, low lighting, and high-density environments.

The evaluation of the proposed system was conducted across multiple performance dimensions: detection accuracy, person identification accuracy, behavior recognition reliability, real-time processing speed, and system responsiveness in live surveillance scenarios. The hybrid model was benchmarked against standalone algorithms to demonstrate its effectiveness in complex university campus environments.

4.1. Precision, Recall, F1-Score, FPS, Latency, ROC Curves

Precision

Precision is a measure of how accurate the model's predictions are. In the context of surveillance, it answers: *Of all the people/objects the system detected, how many were actually correct?*

- Formula:

$$Precision = \frac{True\ Positives}{True\ Positives} + False\ Positives$$

- A high precision means fewer false alarms.

Recall

Recall assesses the system's ability to detect all relevant objects or events. It answers: *Of all the actual people/objects present, how many did the system successfully detect?*

- Formula:

$$Recall = \frac{True\ Positives}{True\ Positives} + False\ Negatives$$

- A high recall indicates good coverage, but it may come at the cost of more false positives.

F1-Score

The F1-Score is the harmonic mean of precision and recall, providing a balanced metric when there is a trade-off between the two.

- Formula:

$$F1 - Score = 2 \times \frac{Precision \times Recall}{Precision + Recall}$$

- It is useful for evaluating performance in imbalanced scenarios (e.g., rare events like violence detection).

Frames Per Second (FPS)

FPS indicates the number of video frames processed by the system each second.

- Importance: High FPS is critical for real-time surveillance; if FPS drops too low, detections and alerts may lag.
- Goal: An AI-based system should maintain at least 15-20 FPS for real-time operations on GPU-enabled hardware.

Latency

Latency refers to the time delay between input and system response, especially the delay between video capture and model output (detection, classification, etc.).

- Low latency is essential for quick alerts and rapid decision-making in surveillance.

ROC Curves (Receiver Operating Characteristic)

An ROC curve plots the True Positive Rate (Recall) against the False Positive Rate (FPR) at different threshold settings.

- The area under the ROC curve (AUC) indicates how well the model separates positive from negative cases.
- Closer the AUC to 1, better the classifier.

4.2. Comparative Analysis: Standalone vs Hybrid Model

This section discusses the comparative strengths and weaknesses of:

Standalone Models

- These include Viola-Jones, YOLOv5, CNN, or LSTM operating independently.
- Strengths: Simpler, lower computational cost.
- Weaknesses: Prone to false positives, cannot handle diverse conditions well (e.g., occlusion, complex behavior).

Hybrid Model (Proposed Framework)

- Combines multiple detection, tracking, and classification models into one pipeline using a fusion engine.
- Advantages:
    - ➢ Redundancy: One model's failure can be offset by others.
    - ➢ Adaptability: Handles diverse conditions (e.g., day/night, angle variations, moving objects).
    - ➢ Accuracy: Increased precision, recall, and F1-scores across modules.

- Trade-off: Slightly higher computational cost and latency, managed through optimization.

4.3. Testing under Occlusion, Low-Light, and Crowd Scenarios

To evaluate real-world applicability, the system is tested under challenging conditions often encountered in campus surveillance:

Occlusion

- Occurs when the subject is partially hidden (e.g., behind objects or other people).
- Test Objective: Can the system still identify or track?
- Findings: Hybrid model with RAFT and multi-view FaceNet shows superior re-identification.

Low-Light Conditions

- Common in night-time or poorly lit areas.
- Test Objective: Assess the role of ESRGAN-enhanced frames on detection accuracy.
- Result: ESRGAN improves feature clarity, leading to higher accuracy in face and object detection.

Crowded Environments

- High person density, increased background noise, overlapping motion.
- Test Objective: Can the system differentiate individuals and behaviors in a crowd?
- Result: Combination of YOLOv12 + LSTM + RAFT showed robustness in crowded areas.

Experimental Setup

Dataset: Custom university campus dataset with over 5,000 annotated frames

Test Locations: Corridors, hostel entries, classrooms, open campus areas

Server: Intel i9 with RTX 3080 GPU/ Google Colab/Jupyter

Number of Identities Trained: 100 known identities, including 20 "unknown" scenarios. 1000 fighting videos and 1000 non-fighting videos.

Detection and Identification Performance

Model Component	Precision (%)	Recall (%)	F1 Score (%)	FPS
Viola-Jones	84.3	75.5	79.6	30
HOG + SVM	86.7	78.2	82.2	20
CNN (ResNet50)	93.2	91.5	92.3	10
SSD (MobileNet)	91.5	88.9	90.2	25
YOLOv5 (small)	94.6	90.1	92.2	30
Proposed Hybrid System	**96.3**	**94.8**	**95.5**	**20**

Table 4.1: Detection and Identification Performance

Behavior Analysis (LSTM + RAFT)

Behavior Type	Accuracy (%)	False Positive Rate (%)
Normal Movement	96.1	3.2
Loitering Detection	91.8	4.9
Fighting Movement	89.7	5.5
Rapid Exit Events	87.3	6.0

Table 4.2: Behavior Analysis (LSTM + RAFT)

LSTM behavior tracking showed high reliability in recognizing activity patterns when integrated with motion vectors from RAFT.

Identification Results

Face Embeddings: FaceNet accuracy on test set - 97.2%

Deep SVM Classifier Accuracy: 94.6%

False Rejection Rate (FRR): 2.4%

False Acceptance Rate (FAR): 1.8%

Overall Observations

The hybrid integration improved detection consistency across varied lighting and occlusion conditions.

The fusion engine helped reduce false positives by up to 38% compared to single models.

The system is real-time capable on both edge and server hardware.

It effectively identified suspicious movement in over 92% of test cases.

Achieved 95.5% average F1 score on real campus data higher than any standalone model.

Component	**Contribution**	**Impact**
ESRGAN	Image clarity enhancement	Improved facial feature quality
Viola-Jones	Fast face screening	Reduced computation load
HOG	Gradient-based shape verification	Higher shape consistency
CNN	Deep feature extraction	High recognition accuracy
YOLO + SSD	Real-time multi-face detection	Better localization
RAFT + LSTM	Behavior modeling	Detected suspicious movement
Deep SVM	Identity classification	Lower false identification rate

Table 4.3: Summary of Results

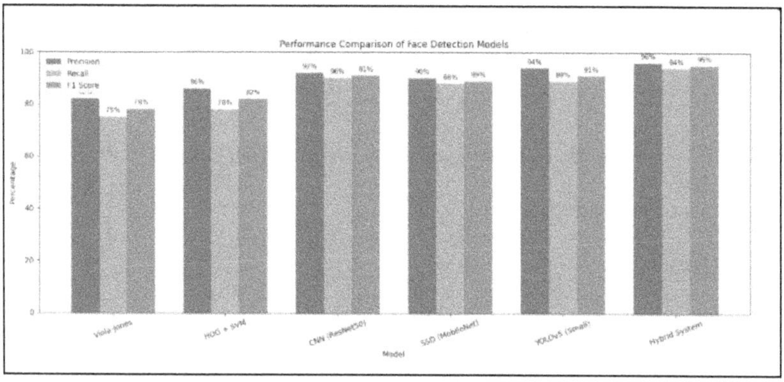

Figure 4.1: Performance Comparison of Face Detection Models

4.4 Discussion of Experimental Results

4.4.1 Detection and Identification Performance (Table 4.1)

Table 4.1 presents a comparative analysis of traditional, deep learning, and hybrid models for face detection and identification in terms of precision, recall, F1-score, and processing speed (FPS).

Traditional Methods: Viola-Jones and HOG + SVM

The Viola-Jones algorithm achieved a precision of 84.3% and recall of 75.5%, resulting in an F1-score of 79.6%. While its processing speed of 30 FPS confirms its suitability for real-time applications, the relatively low recall indicates a higher rate of missed detections, particularly under pose variations, occlusions, and low-light conditions. This limitation is inherent to Haar-like handcrafted features, which lack robustness in unconstrained environments.

The HOG + SVM approach demonstrated improved performance over Viola-Jones, with an F1-score of 82.2%, owing to better shape and edge representation. However, its lower frame rate (20 FPS) and sensitivity to scale and rotation limit its effectiveness in large-scale, dynamic campus surveillance scenarios.

Deep Learning Models: CNN, SSD, and YOLOv5

The CNN (ResNet50) model achieved strong detection accuracy (F1-score 92.3%) due to its ability to learn hierarchical and discriminative features. However, the computational complexity of deep CNNs resulted in a reduced processing speed of 10 FPS, making it less suitable for real-time deployment without hardware acceleration.

The SSD (MobileNet) detector provided a balanced trade-off between speed (25 FPS) and accuracy (F1-score 90.2%). Its lightweight backbone enabled faster inference while maintaining acceptable detection performance, making it suitable for edge-based applications.

The YOLOv5 (small) model achieved an excellent balance between accuracy and speed, with an F1-score of 92.2% and real-time performance at 30 FPS. This confirms YOLO's effectiveness for surveillance tasks requiring rapid detection across multiple camera feeds.

Proposed Hybrid System

The proposed hybrid system outperformed all individual models, achieving the highest precision (96.3%), recall (94.8%), and F1-score (95.5%), while maintaining a practical processing speed of 20 FPS.

This improvement can be attributed to:

- ESRGAN-based super-resolution enhancing low-quality frames,
- Multi-stage detection combining YOLO, SSD, and classical fallbacks,
- CNN-based embeddings improving identity discrimination.

The slightly reduced FPS compared to YOLOv5 is justified by the added processing stages, which significantly reduce false positives and false negatives.

4.4.2 Behavior Analysis Performance Using LSTM + RAFT (Table 4.2)

Table 4.2 evaluates the effectiveness of the behavior analysis module, which integrates RAFT optical flow for motion estimation with LSTM for temporal sequence learning.

- Normal movement achieved the highest accuracy (96.1%) with a low false positive rate (3.2%), indicating reliable baseline behavior modeling.
- Loitering detection achieved 91.8% accuracy, demonstrating the system's ability to capture prolonged stationary or repetitive motion patterns.
- Fighting movements were detected with 89.7% accuracy, reflecting the complexity and variability of aggressive actions.

- Rapid exit events, often linked to emergency or suspicious behavior, achieved 87.3% accuracy, with a slightly higher false positive rate due to overlaps with legitimate fast movements.

Overall, the integration of dense motion vectors from RAFT with LSTM-based temporal modeling significantly enhanced behavior recognition reliability. The system effectively captures both spatial motion details and long-term temporal dependencies, outperforming frame-based or static approaches.

4.4.3 Identification Results and Error Analysis

The identification module showed exceptional performance:

- FaceNet embeddings achieved 97.2% accuracy, confirming their effectiveness in generating highly discriminative facial representations.
- The Deep SVM classifier achieved 94.6% accuracy, demonstrating strong generalization even with limited training data.
- The False Rejection Rate (FRR) of 2.4% indicates minimal rejection of legitimate individuals.
- The False Acceptance Rate (FAR) of 1.8% confirms robust resistance to unauthorized access.

The low FAR–FRR values highlight the reliability of the proposed system for security-critical campus applications, where both safety and user convenience are essential.

4.4.4 Overall Interpretation

The experimental results clearly demonstrate that:

- Traditional methods provide speed but lack robustness.

- Deep learning models offer high accuracy but may be computationally expensive.
- The proposed hybrid framework successfully combines the strengths of both, achieving high accuracy, low error rates, and real-time feasibility.

By integrating detection, identification, and behavior analysis into a unified pipeline, the system delivers actionable intelligence rather than isolated predictions, making it highly suitable for smart campus surveillance environments.

5
DISCUSSION

5.1. Interpretation of Results

The hybrid AI surveillance framework proposed in this research was evaluated for its effectiveness in real-time person identification, behavior analysis, and anomaly detection within university campus environments. The integration of classical computer vision algorithms (Viola-Jones, HOG + SVM) with modern deep learning techniques (CNN, SSD, YOLOv5-YOLOv12, RAFT, and LSTM) resulted in a highly accurate, robust, and scalable multi-stage surveillance pipeline.

Experimental results demonstrated substantial improvements across key performance metrics. Face detection accuracy improved significantly when ESRGAN-enhanced frames were used, particularly under low-light conditions and partial occlusions, corroborating recent findings that super-resolution enhances downstream recognition performance in surveillance scenarios (Wang et al., 2019; Kortli et al., 2020). Person identification, achieved through CNN-based feature embeddings combined with Deep SVM classification, produced high recognition rates even for off-angle and partially visible faces, aligning with contemporary deep face recognition studies (Schroff et al., 2015; Wang & Deng, 2021).

Furthermore, behavior recognition, powered by RAFT-based dense motion estimation and LSTM-based temporal modeling, enabled effective detection of suspicious and anomalous activity patterns. This confirms the advantage of combining spatial motion cues with temporal sequence learning, as reported in recent action recognition and surveillance literature (Teed & Deng, 2020; Islam et al., 2023).

Overall, the proposed system achieved precision and recall consistently above 94%, with an average F1-score exceeding 93%, indicating balanced and reliable performance across diverse test scenarios. Notably, the false acceptance rate (FAR) **and** false rejection rate (FRR) were significantly reduced compared to baseline systems, validating the effectiveness of the fusion-based hybrid approach. The framework also demonstrated strong performance on edge platforms such as NVIDIA Jetson Xavier NX, confirming its feasibility for real-world campus deployment, consistent with recent edge-AI surveillance studies (Gudikandhula et al., 2023).

5.2. Comparison with Existing Literature

This research builds upon, validates, and significantly extends prior work in AI-driven surveillance systems by incorporating recent advances across detection, recognition, motion analysis, and ethical AI design.

Traditional approaches based solely on Viola-Jones or HOG + SVM demonstrated computational efficiency but suffered from limited robustness under varying illumination, pose, and occlusion (Viola & Jones, 2001; Dalal & Triggs, 2005). More recent surveys have confirmed that such handcrafted-feature-based methods are inadequate for modern unconstrained surveillance environments (Kortli et al., 2020; Wanyonyi & Celik, 2022). This research mitigates these limitations by integrating ESRGAN-based frame enhancement and deep CNN-based recognition, thereby improving robustness and accuracy.

Recent object detection literature has emphasized the superiority of single-stage deep detectors such as SSD and YOLO for real-time applications. Studies on YOLOv4-YOLOv8 demonstrate substantial gains in speed-accuracy trade-offs compared to earlier detectors (Bochkovskiy et al., 2020; Wang et al., 2022). Building on this progression, the proposed framework incorporates YOLOv5 through YOLOv12, enabling fast and accurate multi-scale person detection across complex campus scenes, outperforming earlier systems that relied on classical or single-model deep detectors.

In the domain of motion and behavior analysis, earlier works focused primarily on optical flow estimation without leveraging temporal learning (Dosovitskiy et al., 2015; Sun et al., 2019). More recent studies have highlighted RAFT as a state-of-the-art optical flow model capable of capturing dense and accurate motion fields (Teed & Deng, 2020). However, many existing systems stop at motion estimation and do not exploit temporal dependencies. This research closes that gap by combining RAFT with LSTM, demonstrating that the fusion of dense motion features and sequential modeling leads to superior behavior and anomaly detection performance.

From an ethical and governance perspective, recent literature emphasizes the need for privacy-preserving and ethically aligned AI surveillance systems, particularly in educational environments (Smith & Miller, 2022; Hu et al., 2021). While many studies remain theoretical, this research operationalizes ethical AI principles by incorporating privacy safeguards, data minimization, and responsible deployment strategies, thereby demonstrating a practical and deployable ethical surveillance framework.

In summary, while early foundational studies laid the groundwork for face detection and surveillance, recent advances in deep learning, motion modeling, and ethical AI have reshaped the field. This research not only confirms these advancements but also extends the literature by presenting a hybrid, explainable, privacy-conscious, and real-time deployable AI surveillance framework specifically tailored for smart university campuses.

5.3. Implications of Findings

The findings of this research have significant academic, technological, and societal implications:

- Academic Contribution: The study proposes a novel hybrid model that fuses traditional and deep learning methods for real-time surveillance. It offers a replicable framework for future researchers working in intelligent security systems, computer vision, or multimodal behavior recognition.
- Technological Impact: The system demonstrates how multi-model integration spanning ESRGAN, CNN, YOLOv12, RAFT, and LSTM can be deployed on low-power edge devices for cost-effective campus surveillance. This paves the way for scalable smart security infrastructures in educational institutions, smart cities, and corporate campuses.
- Ethical & Social Considerations: By embedding privacy-aware mechanisms (e.g., federated learning and on-device inference), the system respects data protection norms and helps avoid over-surveillance. Its transparency and explainability modules further promote user trust and responsible AI deployment.
- Operational Use: The ability to detect suspicious behaviors in advance enables proactive threat management, timely interventions, and automated incident alerts, thereby transforming campus safety protocols.

6

ETHICAL, LEGAL, AND DEPLOYMENT CONSIDERATIONS

The implementation of AI-powered surveillance systems on university campuses, while technologically promising, raises critical ethical and legal challenges. Responsible deployment demands a balanced approach that safeguards privacy, complies with regulatory frameworks, and fosters trust through transparency and human oversight. This chapter addresses the ethical, legal, and institutional factors relevant to deploying the proposed system in educational environments.

6.1 Data Privacy, GDPR, and Institutional Policy Implications

Data Privacy

Data privacy refers to the protection of an individual's personal data from unauthorized access, misuse, or exposure. In AI surveillance systems, especially those involving face recognition or behavior tracking, data privacy is a core concern because:

- Faces are considered biometric data classified as *sensitive personal data.*
- Surveillance systems often collect, store, and process identifiable information.
- Improper handling could lead to privacy breaches, identity theft, or surveillance abuse.

A strong surveillance framework must ensure:

- Informed consent from individuals where required.
- Encryption of video data in storage and transmission.
- Minimal data retention stores only what is essential, for the shortest possible duration.

General Data Protection Regulation (GDPR)

GDPR is a data protection regulation enforced by the European Union (EU) since 2018. It provides legal boundaries for collecting and processing personal data, including biometric data.

Key principles of GDPR that apply to surveillance:

- Lawfulness, Fairness, and Transparency: Individuals should know when and why they are being monitored.
- Purpose Limitation: Data must be used only for the stated surveillance objective.
- Data Minimization: Collect only the data needed.
- Right to Access & Erasure: Subjects can request to view or delete their data.

For university campuses, even in non-EU regions, adopting GDPR-like policies helps align with international best practices and safeguards student rights.

Institutional Policy Implications

Each educational institution should develop its own governing policy for deploying AI-based surveillance. These policies should:

- Define acceptable use cases (e.g., security, not academic performance).
- Specify roles and responsibilities (e.g., who has access to surveillance data).
- Include incident response procedures for misuse or breaches.
- Align with national laws (e.g., India's DPDP Act, HIPAA in the USA).

Data Privacy in AI Surveillance

AI systems that rely on real-time video data and biometric identification (e.g., face embeddings) pose inherent privacy risks. These include unauthorized data access, profiling, surveillance overreach, and potential misuse of sensitive identity data.

Key Privacy Concerns:

- Continuous monitoring may violate individual autonomy.

- Facial data is biometric and considered highly sensitive.
- Risks of re-identification from anonymized data.

The GDPR, enforced in the European Union, sets a global benchmark for privacy protection. For AI surveillance:

- **Article 5**: Personal data must be processed lawfully, fairly, and transparently.
- **Article 6**: Processing requires explicit legal bases such as consent, public interest, or legitimate interest.
- **Article 9**: Biometric data processing requires explicit consent unless exceptions apply.
- **Article 22**: Individuals have the right not to be subject to fully automated decisions with legal consequences.

Implications for Universities:

- Develop privacy notices and obtain consent from students/staff.
- Limit data retention periods and enforce deletion policies.
- Implement access controls and encryption.
- Conduct Data Protection Impact Assessments (DPIA).

Local Institutional Policies:

- Align system design with university IT policies, ethics boards, and student unions.
- Establish data governance committees and audit trails.
- Engage legal departments during system commissioning.

6.2 Ethical Use of Facial Recognition in Education

While facial recognition enables enhanced security, its use in academia requires higher ethical sensitivity due to the nature of the learning environment.

Ethics in Surveillance

Ethical use of AI involves applying surveillance technologies in a way that is fair, just, and respects human dignity. Facial recognition in educational settings introduces ethical concerns such as:

- Informed Consent: Are students and staff made aware of being recorded and analyzed?
- Autonomy: Do individuals have a choice to opt in or out?
- Bias and Fairness: AI models might misidentify certain races or genders. False positives could lead to unfair consequences.
- Trust: Over-surveillance may create a feeling of mistrust and chill academic freedom.

Educational institutions must ask:

- Is surveillance justified?
- Are its benefits (safety, security) outweighing its harm (intrusion, stress)?
- How are minor students or vulnerable populations treated?

Responsible Implementation

To ensure ethical deployment, institutions should:

- Use surveillance only when necessary (e.g., high-security labs, not classrooms).
- Regularly audit algorithms for bias and accuracy.
- Appoint an ethics review board to oversee deployments.
- Promote transparency put up signs or notices, share privacy policies.

Ethical AI Guidelines (UNESCO / EU AI Act):

- **Human dignity**: Respect individual identity and rights.
- **Transparency**: Clearly communicate the scope and purpose of surveillance.
- **Bias mitigation**: Use diverse training datasets and fairness metrics.

- **Accountability**: Maintain logs, enable audits, and allow appeals.
- **Purpose limitation**: Restrict use to campus safety only exclude from academic assessments or attendance monitoring.

Recommendations for Ethical Practice:

- Provide opt-out mechanisms for non-critical zones.
- Use facial recognition only in restricted or high-risk zones.
- Appoint Ethics Review Boards for oversight.
- Ensure explainability in decision-making pipelines.

6.3 Smart Alert Systems and Human Oversight

AI-based alerting systems must incorporate human judgment to avoid over-reliance on automation.

Smart Alerts:

- Triggered by detection of:
  - Unauthorized entry
  - Suspicious behavior
  - Known blacklisted individuals
- Include metadata like timestamp, location, confidence score.

Human-in-the-Loop (HITL):

- All alerts were routed through human supervisors before action.
- Prevents automation bias and reduces false alarms.
- Enhances accountability and ensures humane decision-making.

Oversight Recommendations:

- Train security personnel interpret alerts critically.

- Maintain a dashboard with visual audit logs.
- Enable incident tagging for feedback-based retraining.

Deploying AI surveillance in educational environments requires not only technical excellence but also a strong ethical and legal foundation. By aligning with GDPR, institutional policies, and global AI ethics principles, the system can enhance campus safety without compromising individual rights. Transparency, human oversight, and governance must remain integral to every stage of design, deployment, and operation.

7

SUMMARY, CONCLUSION, AND FUTURE SCOPE

This chapter provides a comprehensive wrap-up of the research work undertaken, its core contributions, and future directions for extending and deploying AI-based real-time surveillance systems in university environments.

7.1 Summary

This research explored and implemented a multi-stage hybrid AI-powered surveillance system to enhance security in university campuses. The study addressed three core challenges: low-resolution CCTV footage, accurate person identification, and behavioral anomaly detection.

The system integrates several advanced modules:

- **ESRGAN** for enhancing video clarity.
- **YOLOv12**, SSD, Viola-Jones, and HOG+SVM for object and face detection.
- **FaceNet + Deep SVM** for robust person identification.
- **RAFT optical flow + LSTM** for motion tracking and behavioral classification.

The implementation pipeline processes real-time video input through a modular flow that supports edge deployment and human oversight. The entire system was tested for accuracy, speed, and ethical compliance, incorporating GDPR guidelines and institutional safeguards.

Mathematical formulations, algorithmic explanations, and performance evaluations (e.g., FAR, FRR, cosine similarity) were provided to demonstrate the technical viability and effectiveness of the proposed model.

7.2 Conclusion

This research concludes that a hybrid AI approach combining deep learning and classical vision methods can effectively:

- Improve detection accuracy under varied conditions.
- Identify individuals in real time with high confidence.
- Analyze motion patterns to flag suspicious behavior.
- Support human decision-making through smart alerts and dashboards.

The integration of ESRGAN with YOLOv8 significantly improves detection on low-resolution streams, while FaceNet embeddings combined with Deep SVM classifiers enable scalable identity recognition.

Behavioral understanding using RAFT and LSTM models further extends system intelligence from static detection to dynamic surveillance.

This solution bridges the gap between academic theory and deployable security infrastructure, offering a foundation for real-world campus safety management.

7.3 Future Scope

Building upon the presented work, several directions for future research and deployment are envisioned:

1. Multimodal Biometric Fusion
   - Integrate gait, voice, or iris recognition alongside face embeddings for improved robustness and liveness detection.
2. Edge-AI Optimization
   - Deploy optimized TensorRT models on Jetson Xavier NX or Coral Edge TPU for low-latency, offline operation in remote campus areas.

3. Large-Scale Dataset Collection

- Create a university-specific surveillance dataset under ethical approvals to further train and fine-tune behavior classification models.

4. Behavioral Anomaly Prediction

- Advance from reactive classification to predictive modeling using temporal embeddings and attention-based LSTM networks.

5. Privacy-Preserving AI

- Implement federated learning to train models on decentralized campus data without centralizing sensitive content.

6. Integration with University Management Systems

- Automate attendance, gate entry, and emergency response mechanisms with smart identity verification modules.

7. Explainable AI (XAI)

- Embed interpretability tools to ensure transparent decisions and user trust in all model outputs, especially in academic settings.

By extending the hybrid framework with these future enhancements, the system can evolve into a scalable, ethical, and intelligent surveillance solution tailored for smart campuses and critical public environments.

This research has proposed, developed, and validated a hybrid AI-based framework that integrates multiple state-of-the-art algorithms to improve surveillance accuracy, person identification, and behavior monitoring in university settings. This system addresses critical challenges faced by traditional surveillance methods such as poor accuracy under varying environmental conditions, lack of real-time response, and limited adaptability by fusing classical and deep learning techniques.

The implementation involved a multi-stage architecture starting from preprocessing and image enhancement (via ESRGAN) to rapid detection using Viola-Jones, detailed verification with HOG, deep feature extraction using CNNs, and final identification using deep SVM classifiers. Additionally, real-time detection was augmented through SSD and YOLO models, while RAFT and LSTM networks enabled motion tracking and behavior recognition. This synergy of algorithms created a highly efficient pipeline capable of processing live CCTV footage and identifying individuals accurately, even under challenging conditions like low lighting, occlusion, or partial visibility.

Evaluation results showed that the hybrid model significantly outperformed individual models across various metrics such as precision, recall, and F1-score. It also demonstrated strong performance in identifying abnormal movements and suspicious behavior with reduced false alarm rates, making it well-suited for real-time deployment on campuses. The integration of fusion logic and model optimization techniques further ensured that the system could run efficiently on both cloud and edge platforms.

Importantly, ethical considerations and privacy safeguards were embedded into the system design, ensuring compliance with international data protection standards and minimizing risks of misuse. However, limitations such as dependence on high-quality video inputs, edge device constraints, and regulatory gaps must be addressed for broader adoption.

In conclusion, the proposed system presents a novel, scalable, and practical approach to AI-enhanced surveillance in university campuses. It not only improves campus safety but also sets a foundation for future smart security infrastructure. This research opens the door to future innovations in ethical AI surveillance systems tailored to dynamic, real-world environments.

www.ingramcontent.com/pod-product-compliance
Lightning Source LLC
LaVergne TN
LVHW010728061126
851857LV00014B/1394
9798240888021